New Directions for Community Colleges

Arthur M. Cohen
EDITOR-IN-CHIEF

Richard L. Wagoner
ASSOCIATE EDITOR

Gabriel Jones
MANAGING EDITOR

Contemporary Issues in Institutional Ethics

Clifford P. Harbour
Patricia L. Farrell
EDITORS

Number 148 • Winter 2009
Jossey-Bass
San Francisco

CONTEMPORARY ISSUES IN INSTITUTIONAL ETHICS
Clifford P. Harbour, Patricia L. Farrell (eds.)
New Directions for Community Colleges, no. 148

Arthur M. Cohen, Editor-in-Chief
Richard L. Wagoner, Associate Editor
Gabriel Jones, Managing Editor

NEW DIRECTIONS FOR COMMUNITY COLLEGES (ISSN 0194-3081, electronic ISSN 1536-0733) is part of The Jossey-Bass Higher and Adult Education Series and is published quarterly by Wiley Subscription Services, Inc., A Wiley Company, at Jossey-Bass, 989 Market Street, San Francisco, CA 94103-1741. Periodicals Postage Paid at San Francisco, CA, and at additional mailing offices. POSTMASTER: Send address changes to New Directions for Community Colleges, Jossey-Bass, 989 Market Street, San Francisco, CA 94103-1741.

SUBSCRIPTIONS cost $98.00 for individuals and $269.00 for institutions, agencies, and libraries in the United States. Prices subject to change.

EDITORIAL CORRESPONDENCE should be sent to the Editor-in-Chief, Arthur M. Cohen, at the Graduate School of Education and Information Studies, University of California, Box 951521, Los Angeles, CA 90095-1521. All manuscripts receive anonymous reviews by external referees.

New Directions for Community Colleges is indexed in CIJE: Current Index to Journals in Education (ERIC), Contents Pages in Education (T&F), Current Abstracts (EBSCO), Ed/Net (Simpson Communications), Education Index/Abstracts (H. W. Wilson), Educational Research Abstracts Online (T&F), ERIC Database (Education Resources Information Center), and Resources in Education (ERIC).

Microfilm copies of issues and articles are available in 16mm and 35mm, as well as microfiche in 105mm, through University Microfilms Inc., 300 North Zeeb Road, Ann Arbor, MI 48106-1346.

CONTENTS

EDITORS' NOTES   1
Clifford P. Harbour, Patricia L. Farrell

1. Negotiating the Community College Institutional   5
Accountability Environment: A Deweyan Perspective
Clifford P. Harbour, Michael Day
The authors pose an ethical dilemma resulting from the application of
a state institutional accountability program and explain how specific
principles from John Dewey's philosophy of education may help vali-
date the importance of priorities not captured by commitments to open
access and the comprehensive mission.

2. Prepared for Challenges: The Importance of a Professional   17
and Institutional Ethical Identity
Sharon K. Anderson, Linda Lujan, Diane L. Hegeman
This chapter furthers the discussion of a framework for professional
ethical identity development for community college leaders by propos-
ing an "institutional ethical identity" framework.

3. Ethical Dimensions of the Open-Door Admissions Policy   31
William G. Ingram, Sharon E. Morrissey
The authors, community college presidents in North Carolina, explain
how critical issues concerning the community college open-door policy may emerge and test values at the center of the institution's mission
when working with resident undocumented adult learners.

4. Diversity-Affirming Ethics and Critical Epistemology: 39
Institutional Decision Making in Community Colleges
Antonette Aragon, Edward J. Brantmeier
This chapter raises awareness about a potential approach to institutional decision making in community colleges that embody diversity-
affirming ethics and a critical epistemological orientation that promotes
social justice.

5. Ethical Issues for Community College Student Affairs   53
Professionals
Anne M. Hornak
This chapter presents an overview of student affairs in community colleges, including developmental theories related to ethical and moral
development, a review of the major ethical codes and standards for
student affairs professionals, and a framework for resolving ethical
dilemmas.

6. Ethics in an Online Environment   63
Regina L. Garza Mitchell
The blending of technology and education introduces unique ethical dilemmas that have collegewide implications. This author addresses ethical issues with the online education environment such as the use of electronic materials and privacy.

7. An Inquiry Process for Individual and Institutional Ethics   71
Patricia L. Farrell
This final chapter provides a process for inquiring into institutional ethics because, as Dewey noted, inquiry regarding institutional ethics must be continuous and open-ended.

INDEX   79

EDITORS' NOTES

Community colleges exist in an increasingly complex environment characterized by constant change and a range of conflicting academic, community, political, and financial responsibilities. Campus leaders, faculty, and staff are often called on to make decisions that balance interests and concerns framed by these considerations. Often these decisions have an ethical component. College personnel may be able to turn to a rich literature that addresses the relevant academic, community, political, and financial dimensions of specific problems. However, the literature on the ethical dimensions of institutional decision making by community college professionals is limited.

The purpose of this volume is to examine the ethical dimensions of various institutional issues, policies, and practices at the community college. Accordingly, the volume focuses on topics that have an important ethical component that transcends specific program areas, campus services, and leadership positions. Thus the intent is not to address the ethical dilemmas encountered by individual community college presidents, deans, or faculty members but rather to focus on the ethical dimensions of complex problems affecting a variety of college employees and offices. This emphasis on institutional ethics (and not the professional ethical responsibilities of specific individuals) makes the volume relevant to a wide audience. We believe that it will also contribute to the development of ethical professional practice throughout the institution.

The target audience for this volume includes community college administrators, faculty, staff, and governing boards. Faculty teaching courses in higher education policy, leadership, curriculum, diversity, and student affairs will find the volume relevant for their master's and doctoral students. But more important, we picture this volume being used as a tool for individuals on campus and within their own units to dialogue, reflect on, and come to a common understanding of the ethical dimensions of their work with the students, board, and community.

In Chapter One, Harbour and Day discuss specific principles from John Dewey's philosophy on education and offer a foundation that permits us to understand the community college's responsibility to educate adults in a democratic society. The authors examine a hypothetical ethical dilemma posed by application of a state institutional accountability program. They explain how a community college president whose college is expected to meet the state accountability mandates might prioritize this responsibility with respect to critical responsibilities not captured by commitments to open access and the comprehensive mission.

NEW DIRECTIONS FOR COMMUNITY COLLEGES, no. 148, Winter 2009 © 2009 Wiley Periodicals, Inc.
Published online in Wiley InterScience (www.interscience.wiley.com) • DOI: 10.1002/cc.381

Community colleges are diverse places of employment, and the focus on congruency of the college's mission and values is rarely discussed by all involved in the institution. In Chapter Two, Anderson, Lujan, and Hegeman expand on previous work regarding professional ethical identity development to explain how community college leaders should contribute to the development of an "institutional ethical identity" by using the same individual concepts and strategies but at the institutional level. Consciously creating an institution's ethical identity and promoting opportunities for employees' ethical acculturation provides the impetus for shared values and ethics that result in beneficial change in the college culture.

Offering universal or open access has been a preeminent part of community colleges' missions since their beginnings in the early 1900s. Ingram and Morrissey address open access in Chapter Three through a range of institutional ethical assumptions and issues concerning the admission of undocumented immigrants.

In Chapter Four, Aragon and Brantmeier argue eloquently that community colleges hold the potential to provide the catalyst for profound social change because of their mission of open access and thus are most capable of leveling and transforming the playing field for the historically marginalized. The authors propose new conversations about how a diversity-affirming ethical orientation and how an understanding of critical epistemology might influence institutional decision making toward social justice.

Community colleges emphasize teaching and learning in the traditional classroom, on-line learning, and outreach efforts. Behind the scenes are individuals who assist students with their courses, financial aid, and personal issues. These individuals encounter ethical dilemmas each time they meet with a student. In Chapter Five, Hornak addresses ethical responsibilities and standards of student services personnel at community colleges by providing a background on student developmental theories related to ethical and moral development, an overview of the major ethical codes and standards for student affairs professionals, and a framework for resolving ethical dilemmas.

Examining and talking about ethical issues in a community college must be ongoing because today's world is complex and ever-changing. The blending of technology and education introduces unique ethical dilemmas that have collegewide implications. In Chapter Six, Garza Mitchell attends to ethical issues with the online education environment, including institutional policies for teaching and the use of copyrighted materials and other intellectual property.

Collectively, the authors have set out to explore various ethical dilemmas that faculty, administrators, and staff encounter every day at their colleges based on the diverse issues of the early twenty-first century. We do not attempt to address all areas or issues that might give rise to ethical dilemmas at today's community college. However, we hope that the stories, vignettes, and scenarios presented by the contributors to this volume help illuminate and explain critical ethical decisions with the goal of helping college personnel explore, learn, and develop an institutional ethical identity as introduced by Anderson, Lujan, and Hegeman in Chapter Two. In the final chapter, Farrell provides a process for inquiring into institutional ethics because, as Dewey noted back in 1938, inquiry regarding institutional ethics must be continuous and open-ended.

As an aid to further discussion, guiding questions are provided at the end of each chapter.

Clifford P. Harbour
Patricia L. Farrell
Editors

Reference

Dewey, J. *Logic: The Theory of Inquiry.* New York: Holt, Rinehart and Winston, 1938.

CLIFFORD P. HARBOUR *is associate professor in the adult and postsecondary education program at the University of Wyoming.*

PATRICIA L. FARRELL *is the director of university outreach and policy research at the Presidents Council, State Universities of Michigan.*

NEW DIRECTIONS FOR COMMUNITY COLLEGES • DOI: 10.1002/cc

1

Institutional accountability programs may present ethical dilemmas for community college leaders. Some of these dilemmas may be resolved by relying on the authority of the traditional mission. However, in some instances, the mission may be inadequate to check this form of state encroachment. We propose that campus leaders review John Dewey's philosophy of education to gain insights into how their institutions might negotiate dilemmas not addressed by the traditional mission.

Negotiating the Community College Institutional Accountability Environment: A Deweyan Perspective

Clifford P. Harbour, Michael Day

Community college leaders face a wide range of ethical challenges in managing their institutions. One of these challenges is negotiating the various accountability expectations imposed on the institution. Traditionally, community colleges were formally accountable through their governing boards to state legislatures, local voters, and the community for the proper expenditure of funds, administration of relevant state or local policies, and implementation of the institutional mission. However, the 1980s marked the beginning of a new era when state legislatures began systematically to create new accountability expectations concerning institutional performance.

State institutional accountability programs have been classified as first-generation or second-generation (see Harbour and Jaquette, 2007). First-generation accountability programs include performance-reporting, performance-budgeting, and performance-funding initiatives (Burke, 2005). These programs typically require that institutions report their achievements on specific performance measures (such as student graduation rates, student transfer rates, and student pass rates on certain licensure examinations). Under performance-funding and performance-budgeting programs, some portion of state funding is linked directly (with respect to performance funding) or indirectly (with respect to performance budgeting) to institutional performance. Second-generation accountability mechanisms allocate some portion of state funding through market-based mechanisms such as

NEW DIRECTIONS FOR COMMUNITY COLLEGES, no. 148, Winter 2009 © 2009 Wiley Periodicals, Inc.
Published online in Wiley InterScience (www.interscience.wiley.com) • DOI: 10.1002/cc.382

vouchers, institution-specific performance contracts, or fee-for-service contracts (Newman, Couturier, and Scurry, 2004). First-generation programs attempt to hold institutions accountable to the state (operating as a regulator) through assessment of performance on specific measures. Second-generation programs attempt to hold institutions accountable to the state (operating as a consumer) by creating market incentives to improve efficiency and effectiveness on various outcomes identified in legislation or state contracts.

Research on the effectiveness of first-generation programs at community colleges is still very limited, although there are some exceptions (see Dougherty and Hong, 2006). The novelty of second-generation programs, at least in the United States, has precluded significant research on them. What can be discerned at this point, however, are the stated purposes of both first-generation and second-generation programs. That is, whether aimed at community colleges or other public colleges and universities, these programs are designed to influence institutions to meet certain legislatively mandated outcomes through either regulatory or market mechanisms. When success or failure in meeting these outcomes has significant financial consequences, institutional leaders and governing boards may be forced to treat them as priorities of equal or greater importance when compared to other accountability expectations identified by the state, the governing board, the institution, or the academy. In some cases, these expectations may become a de facto mission for an institution (Harbour, 2006). What lies behind many first-generation and second-generation accountability programs is the fundamental assumption that higher education is now a business and that institutions should be driven, at least to some extent, by politically defined economic values such as profit, efficiency, and performance on measurable outcomes (Harbour, 2006).

The implementation of state-mandated institutional accountability programs has raised new ethical dilemmas for community college leaders. For example, it is easy to imagine how campus leaders might struggle in implementing their mission-driven responsibility to promote greater access to higher education while attempting to improve institutional performance on accountability expectations such as improved graduation and transfer rates. That is, enrollment of an expanding underprepared student population might undermine a community college's efforts to focus resources on preparing students for graduation and transfer. We believe, however, that the ethical dilemmas precipitated by state accountability mandates would be especially difficult when these expectations threaten responsibilities we typically associate with community colleges but seldom see inscribed in the mission (for example, the responsibility for educating adults to take their place in a democracy).

With this in mind, we construct and critically examine an ethical dilemma within the context of a vignette to show how the central principles of a community college's mission, open access and the comprehensive curriculum (Vaughan, 1985) may be insufficient to help campus leaders in resolving some ethical dilemmas precipitated by accountability mandates. We argue that this shortcoming shows that community colleges need a more explicit mission that affirms some important responsibilities typically associated with public higher education but not inscribed in the traditional mission. More specifically, in an era of increasing marketization in public higher education, we contend that the community college mission needs to affirm the limited but critically important role of community colleges in educating an adult population capable of supporting a democratic society. To develop our argument, we review some of John Dewey's work to show how it could help community college leaders address such dilemmas. We believe that Dewey's work opens the door to serious consideration of a modification of the mission to include explicit language encouraging community colleges to assume a more vigorous role in preparing adult learners to take their place in the American democracy.

To accomplish these tasks, we have organized our discussion in the following manner. First, we present a vignette that poses an ethical dilemma precipitated by a state institutional accountability mandate. Second, we review Dewey's discussion regarding democracy, education, and educational objectives as set forth in *Democracy and Education* (Dewey, 2008a).Third, after distilling the central points from Dewey's text, we explain how they can help community college leaders in resolving ethical dilemmas like the one presented in our vignette. Finally, we explain how a Deweyan revision of the traditional community college mission would help community college leaders in securing their institution's role in educating adults prepared to participate in a democratic society.

The Dilemma

Linda Lucero has just completed her third year as president of Mountain and Plains Community College (MPCC). MPCC is a publicly supported community college with a mission statement explicitly committing the institution to open access and a comprehensive curriculum. President Lucero has taken significant steps to renew the campus culture of shared governance and expand the college's academic and vocational programs. These efforts resulted in a more positive organizational climate, improved collaboration with the community, and an increase in student enrollment. The increase in enrollment has produced the best budget ever: MPCC now receives $20 million in enrollment funding each year from the state, a substantial base for the college's overall budget of $30 million.

President Lucero's biggest challenge heading into her fourth year revolves around the state's institutional accountability program for community colleges. Five years ago, the state legislature passed a law that linked additional state funding to institutional performance. The state's community college system office is now required to measure each college's annual performance on ten indicators and then allocate the performance funds using a formula. The formula purports to allocate these monies based on the number of "superior" ratings colleges receive on the ten indicators. Ten superior ratings would result in a college's receiving 100 percent of the performance funding for which it was eligible. No superior ratings would result in a college's receiving 0 percent of the performance funding for which it was eligible. Given the size of MPCC, this means it could receive approximately $3 million each year in additional funding if it scores in the superior category on all ten indicators.

During Lucero's first two years as president, MPCC scored in the superior category for all ten indicators, and by the third year, the $3 million in additional funding was regarded by many on campus as more or less permanent. At the end of that year, however, MPCC scored superior in only seven of the ten categories, and its budget was consequently reduced by almost $1 million. In light of this reduction, President Lucero asked the vice president for administration to lead a performance task force to investigate the new lower ratings and propose solutions. The task force found that the lower ratings were primarily due to reduced licensure pass rates for students graduating from the associate degree nursing program, the law enforcement training program, and especially the real estate licensure (REL) program. The task force also noted that student enrollment in the REL program exceeded the enrollment in all other licensure programs combined.

The task force offered two recommendations. The first was to add two new full-time instructors to the REL program and thereby improve instruction and the likelihood that more students would pass the licensure exam. The second recommendation was to close the MPCC Humanities Learning Community (HLC) program. The HLC program was an initiative within the Arts and Sciences division that scheduled and staffed college-level humanities courses open to all degree-seeking transfer and vocational students. Last year, the HLC program and its two full-time faculty members received special mention from a program review team of humanities faculty at other state community colleges. The program review team identified two particular strengths. First, the HLC program had implemented teaching and learning strategies in selected humanities courses specially designed to nurture and support democratic values such as community engagement, tolerance, collaboration, and respect for diversity. Second, the HLC program encouraged students to develop their own learning programs, which appeared related to lower course attrition rates when compared to humanities courses at other community colleges in the state.

Despite this positive review, the task force concluded that all of the HLC program's humanities courses could be cut and equivalents offered through adjunct staffing. Consequently, the best use of MPCC's resources would require elimination of the HLC program, dismissing the two HLC faculty, and using these resources to hire two new full-time instructors for the REL program. This, the task force reasoned, would best enable MPCC to regain its superior ratings under the state accountability program and thereby receive additional performance funding.

We suggest that there are three likely frameworks that President Lucero might use to analyze the task force recommendations. First, if she thinks of MPCC as a business, she might analyze the recommendation based on its consequences for increased revenue and service to her institution's customers. Under this framework, open access and the comprehensive mission are important principles, but securing MPCC's revenue stream would be the dominant consideration in making her decision. Second, President Lucero might base her analysis on the consequences for open access. Accordingly, she might consider whether implementation of the recommendation would increase or decrease the funding allocated to MPCC and thereby enable the college to secure and expand enrollment, an important factor but certainly not the only one in considering open access. Third, MPCC's president might approach the dilemma by considering its consequences for the comprehensive curriculum. This approach would lead President Lucero to study how implementation of the recommendations might help or hinder MPCC in securing or expanding its program offerings.

Obviously, our dilemma does not capture the full chaos and complexity that attends such decisions. However, the purpose in posing the dilemma and these frameworks is to make two points. First, because the MPCC mission statement includes explicit commitments to open access and the comprehensive curriculum, President Lucero has authority she can rely on if she chooses to decline the task force recommendations because of the possible negative consequences for these mission-based priorities. Even though MPCC might lose performance funding by not following the task force recommendations, she has legitimate reasons for putting mission-based priorities ahead of increased state funding. Second, because MPCC's mission does not commit the college to educating adult learners to play a meaningful role in American democracy, President Lucero would be without important authority to justify rejection of the task force recommendations if she thought that the value of the HLC program exceeded the value of the additional performance funding. The irony here is that although we often characterize the community college as "democracy's college," this identification does not typically entail any explicit responsibility to educate students about their role in the democracy under which they live. And absent an explicit statement concerning this responsibility, programs and services that accomplish this goal might be sacrificed, especially in circumstances where funding is a critical issue.

Discussion

We believe that community colleges need to be guided by more than commitments to open access, the comprehensive curriculum, and state accountability mandates. For example, Dowd (2003) observed that if community colleges are to be justifiably regarded as "democracy's college," they should also be committed to equitable outcomes (such as progress toward greater equity between students of different races and socioeconomic groups in earning degrees or transferring to a senior institution). Following Dowd, Harbour and Jaquette (2007) contended that equitable outcomes are so important that states should use funding incentives to attain them.

Our purpose here is not to argue for the adoption of equitable outcomes as a part of the mission or to say what these equitable outcomes might be. We only note that there is a developing line of argument in the literature that claims community colleges should be guided by more than their traditional commitments to open access and the comprehensive curriculum.

We contend that one of these principles should be recognition of the institution's responsibility to educate adults to play a meaningful role in a democratic society. And we contend that once this principle is incorporated into the mission, this would enable college leaders such as President Lucero to approach dilemmas like the one posed in our vignette more directly. Of course, an understanding of what it would mean to help adult learners develop this capacity requires some discussion of what we mean by democracy, education, and the appropriate objectives or aims that should be developed in this activity. To develop these points, we turn to John Dewey.

Dewey on Democracy, Education, and Educational Aims. Any attempt to identify Dewey's position on educational issues must note three significant qualifications. First, the majority of Dewey's work on education concerned elementary and secondary education. Although community colleges were just emerging at the time of Dewey's death in 1952, Dewey scholars (including Westbrook, 1991, and Pappas, 2008) clearly affirm that his texts articulate important principles concerning adult learning and the purpose of education in American democracy.

Second, when Dewey did discuss two-year colleges, this occurred at a time (1902–1903) when these institutions were in their infancy and outnumbered by private, nonprofit two-year institutions (Cohen and Brawer, 2008; Dewey, 2008b, 2008c). Accordingly, there are very few references to two-year institutions in his work (and no substantive references to community colleges). The two significant instances in which two-year colleges were mentioned were in texts examining the education of women (Dewey, 2008b) and the curriculum of the College of Education at the University of Chicago (Dewey, 2008c).

Third, there are several broad themes that run through Dewey's work that might be used to develop a Deweyan approach to educational issues. For example, one might focus on Dewey's writings on inquiry (Johnston, 2006) and its implications for curriculum and pedagogy. A second approach might examine Dewey's views on technology and its relevance to teaching and learning (Hickman, 1990). For purposes of this chapter, however, we have focused on selected principles developed in some of Dewey's writing on democracy and education (Dewey, 2008a; see also Westbrook, 1991, and Pappas, 2008). Attention to this area of focus illuminates Dewey's commitment to education in a democracy and the ethical implications for how and why instruction should be delivered.

Given these qualifications, we use Dewey's (2008a) landmark text *Democracy and Education* as the basis for our work, most specifically his discussion of educational purposes or, in the language he uses, "educational aims." We select this text for several reasons. First, *Democracy and Education* has been recognized as Dewey's "most important book on education" (Westbrook, 1991, p. 168). Second, Ryan (1995) indicates that Dewey regarded the book as the one coming closest to providing an overall account of his philosophy. Most important, however, Dewey's preface to *Democracy and Education* reveals its suitability as a foundation to articulate principles that may guide community college leaders when facing dilemmas such as the one posed in our vignette. There Dewey promised readers that the pages of the text "embody an endeavor to detect and state the ideas implied in a democratic society and to apply these ideas to the problems of the enterprise of education" (2008a, p. 3).

To begin with, Dewey's conceptualization of what education should be was closely tied to his vision of a democratic society. For Dewey, "a democracy is more than a form of government; it is primarily a mode of associated living" (2008a, p. 93). Associated living is characterized by two features. First, when compared to other societies, there are more varied and shared common interests among the people, which in turn promote social stability. By this, Dewey meant that in a democracy, people recognize their common interests and that the desire to secure and promote these larger shared interests leads people to avoid behaviors harmful to others. Second, a democracy enjoys "freer interaction between social groups" and the successful resolution of social challenges as a result of these interactions (p. 92). This passage reflected Dewey's belief that recognition of shared interests and the ability to interact constructively to resolve social challenges leads to a more progressive society and more enlightened inhabitants. Thus Dewey claimed that democracies are noted for "the widening of the area of shared concerns and the liberation of a greater diversity of personal capacities" (p. 93).

As Pappas (2008) noted, for Dewey, democracy required much more than the mere absence of interference or "negative freedom." That is, a democracy required more than freedom from governmental suppression and censorship. For Dewey, democracy also required "positive freedom," which is the development of individuals' intellectual and moral ability to critically assess the environment and then act as members of a community. As Dewey (2008a) noted, a democratic society "must have a type of education which gives individuals a personal interest in social relationships and control, and the habits of mind which secure social changes without introducing disorder" (p. 105).

Turning to his discussion of educational objectives or aims, we note Dewey's observation that "the aim of education is to enable individuals to continue their education" or, as he later stated, "the object and reward of learning is continued capacity for growth" (2008a, p. 107). For Dewey, the primary purpose of education was not to satisfy some need or goal outside of the individual's experience or educational endeavors. Instead, the primary purpose was to help the learner develop. To be sure, the consequences of this development would benefit the learner's family, community, employer, and nation. But these were secondary concerns and not the primary objective of adult learning.

Given this understanding of educational purposes or aims, it is easy to see why Dewey distinguished good aims from bad aims. In his view, good aims had three major qualities. First, a good aim was "an outgrowth of existing conditions" (2008a, p. 111). By this, Dewey meant that a good educational aim was framed by the learner's present condition and the resources or problems encountered. Educational aims, therefore, were not to be directed by a desire to accommodate a theory or some external authority. Second, a good aim was flexible and "capable of alteration to meet circumstances" (p. 111). This quality was essential when developing an aim because for Dewey, a good aim was based on the experiences of the learner, and as these experiences changed, the aim should change as well. Third, a good aim was one that represented "a freeing of activities" and guided, but did not compel, the learner to focus exclusively on the end (p. 112). This claim reflected Dewey's belief that the primary significance of an educational aim was not its role in focusing the learner on a specific end but the long series of learning experiences that lead to the end.

Our discussion of Dewey's work on education, democracy, and educational aims is not offered to suggest that his insights are singularly sufficient to guide the work of community colleges and their leaders in making curricular decisions. However, as an additional source, they may represent an opportunity to recover some balance in the educational process for adult learners. As Grubb and Lazerson (2004) recently explained, the curriculum at higher education institutions, and especially at community colleges, has become dominated by the desire to prepare students for their future role as workers and consumers in the American economy. However, we believe that community college leaders would benefit by approaching many decisions with a view toward how democracy's college might also play a role in helping learners develop themselves as independent citizens in the American democracy. We now explain how aspects of Dewey's work concerning the development of adult learners in a democracy might be placed within the institutional mission beside the historical commitments to open access and comprehensive curricula. We begin by returning to President Lucero's dilemma.

Deweyan Implications for President Lucero. In the dilemma we presented earlier, we argued that the traditional commitments to open access and the comprehensive curriculum provided President Lucero with authority to decline the recommendations made by the MPCC task force. However, commitments to open access and the comprehensive curriculum did not recognize the important responsibility that community colleges have to help develop a population capable of sustaining democracy.

Our point in reviewing Dewey's remarks was not to suggest that community college leaders should discount open access and the comprehensive mission as essential principles in the community college mission. Our point was simply to note the importance of offering adult learners the kinds of experiences that enable them to develop the knowledge and skills appropriate for citizens in a democratic society. The experiences leading to this knowledge and skill should be seen as valuable and may in many cases be more important than the financial rewards allocated to institutions in state accountability programs. Unfortunately, the community college mission typically does not include an explicit statement of this responsibility, and without it, community college leaders lack a valuable tool in checking the growing influence of state mandates that are often more concerned with private sector values such as performance and efficiency. We believe that President Lucero would be in a much better position to make an informed decision if the MPCC mission included language affirming this responsibility and the institution's role as a public sector organization with civic responsibilities. This language would help President Lucero defend initiatives like the HLC program. This language might be as succinct as the following: "MPCC is committed to supporting adult learners in developing their knowledge, skills, and values in ways that are important to them personally and appropriate to the creation on an informed and engaged citizen of the American democracy."

Conclusion

New state accountability programs have created new responsibilities for community colleges. These responsibilities may precipitate ethical dilemmas for college leaders. In some situations, traditional commitments to open access and the comprehensive curriculum provide adequate authority to check the encroachment of state accountability expectations on the greater purposes of the institution. In other cases, however, state accountability mandates pose a threat to important responsibilities we often associate with community colleges but seldom see articulated in their mission statements.

We know that college leaders are ready to defend their colleges' commitment to open access and the comprehensive mission when threatened by such accountability programs. We also believe, however, that many of these same leaders would defend their colleges' work in providing the kind of educational experiences that help students develop in ways most important to them and their democracy if they had suitable language incorporated into their mission statements. Our purpose here was to articulate such language and provide an explanation of how it might be grounded in the work of John Dewey.

Guiding Questions

1. How do campus leaders at your college consider open access and the comprehensive mission in making changes to the curriculum or in making allocations of resources?

NEW DIRECTIONS FOR COMMUNITY COLLEGES • DOI: 10.1002/cc

2. How do campus leaders at your college determine when major ethical issues are relevant to open access and the comprehensive mission?
3. How do faculty members at your college describe the importance of educating students to play a meaningful role in the American democracy? How does this priority compare to other priorities at the college?
4. How do campus leaders at your college assess the importance of state institutional accountability programs and balance their demands against your institution's commitments to open access, the comprehensive mission, and the responsibility to educate adults to play a meaningful role in the American democracy?

References

Burke, J. C. "The Three Corners of the Accountability Triangle: Serving All, Submitting to None." In J. C. Burke (ed.), *Achieving Accountability in Higher Education*. San Francisco: Jossey-Bass, 2005.

Cohen, A. M., and Brawer, F. B. *The American Community College* (5th ed.). San Francisco: Jossey-Bass, 2008.

Dewey, J. "Democracy and Education." In J. A. Boydston (ed.), *The Middle Works of John Dewey, 1899–1924*, Vol. 9. Carbondale: Southern Illinois University Press, 2008a.

Dewey, J. "Memorandum to President Harper on Coeducation." In J. A. Boydston (ed.), *The Middle Works of John Dewey, 1899–1924*, Vol. 2. Carbondale: Southern Illinois University Press, 2008b.

Dewey, J. "The Organization and Curricula of the College of Education." In J. A. Boydston (Ed.), *The Middle Works of John Dewey, 1899–1924*, Vol. 3. Carbondale: Southern Illinois University Press, 2008c.

Dougherty, K. J., and Hong, E. "Performance Accountability as Imperfect Panacea: The Community College Experience." In T. Bailey and V. S. Morest (eds.), *Defending the Community College Equity Agenda*. Baltimore, Md.: Johns Hopkins University Press, 2006.

Dowd, A. "From Access to Outcome Equity: Revitalizing the Democratic Mission of the Community College." *Annals of the American Association for Political and Social Sciences*, 2003, *586*, 92–119.

Grubb, W. N., and Lazerson, M. *The Education Gospel: The Economic Power of Schooling*. Cambridge, Mass.: Harvard University Press, 2004.

Harbour, C. P. "The Incremental Marketization and Centralization of State Control of Public Higher Education: A Hermeneutic Interpretation of Legislative and Administrative Texts." *International Journal of Qualitative Methods*, 2006, *5*(3), art. 4. [http://www.ualberta.ca/~iiqm/backissues/5_3/PDF/harbour.pdf]. Jan. 17, 2007.

Harbour, C. P., and Jaquette, O. "Advancing an Equity Agenda at the Community College in an Age of Privatization, Performance Accountability, and Marketization." *Equity and Excellence in Education*, 2007, *40*, 197–207.

Hickman, L. A. *John Dewey's Pragmatic Technology*. Bloomington: Indiana University Press, 1990.

Johnston, J. S. *Inquiry and Education: John Dewey and the Quest for Democracy*. Albany: State University of New York Press, 2006.

Newman, F., Couturier, L., and Scurry, J. *The Future of Higher Education: Rhetoric, Reality, and the Risks of the Market*. San Francisco: Jossey-Bass, 2004.

Pappas, G. F. *John Dewey's Ethics: Democracy as Experience*. Bloomington: Indiana University Press, 2008.

Ryan, A. *John Dewey and the High Tide of American Liberalism*. New York: Norton, 1995.
Vaughan, G. B. "Maintaining Open Access and Comprehensiveness." In D. Puyear (ed.), *Maintaining Institutional Integrity*. New Directions for Community Colleges, no. 52. San Francisco: Jossey-Bass, 1985.
Westbrook, R. B. *John Dewey and American Democracy*. Ithaca, N.Y.: Cornell University Press, 1991.

CLIFFORD P. HARBOUR is associate professor in the adult and postsecondary education program at the University of Wyoming.

MICHAEL DAY is professor in the adult and postsecondary education program at the University of Wyoming.

2

Anderson, Harbour, and Davies (2007) have proposed a framework of professional identity development for community college leaders. We further this discussion by introducing the idea of "institutional ethical identity" and offer suggestions for how leaders and constituents can work together to build a shared ethical identity on the community college campus.

Prepared for Challenges: The Importance of a Professional and Institutional Ethical Identity

Sharon K. Anderson, Linda Lujan, Diane L. Hegeman

Dr. Alice Farris-Smith was stepping into her first presidency at North Suburban Community College (NSCC), the smallest of three colleges in a local district serving over twenty thousand students per year. She was replacing a president of fourteen years who had become somewhat complacent in his final years. Alice had a solid grounding in community college leadership acquired during her academic training as well as twenty years in academic and student affairs at three different community colleges. The chancellor who hired Alice reported to a seven-person governing board that subscribed to the policy governance model and rarely meddled in operational matters. The chancellor had assured her that NSCC was a good college with normal problems but needed to aggressively seek new programs and partnerships, engage formally and informally with its community, and develop alternative funding streams. Alice was comfortable with this directive and had already decided she would spend her first year building internal relationships and trust while conducting her own analysis of the institution and community.

As Alice started to get to know the college, she began to uncover both positives and negatives in the community college's day-to-day operations. For example, she was pleased to see that NSCC's core value of student success was a primary focus of the college at all levels. However, she also spotted some challenges. In the absence of day-to-day oversight from the former president, the faculty and staff had become accustomed to making most operational decisions. Furthermore, NSCC's enrollments had been declining, and

NEW DIRECTIONS FOR COMMUNITY COLLEGES, no. 148, Winter 2009 © 2009 Wiley Periodicals, Inc.
Published online in Wiley InterScience (www.interscience.wiley.com) • DOI: 10.1002/cc.383

the state and district were dealing with reduced tax revenues resulting in three successive years of college budget cuts. NSCC had several active employee groups advocating tirelessly for constituents' rights as well as a shared governance council that had not convened for the past two years. Finally, Alice detected some community distrust and unease with the college's and district's lack of financial transparency. Given the economic climate in the state and local community, the community questioned how the college spent its money.

At the end of her third month, Alice's signature file contained ten sets of travel authorizations for a two-week mid-December trip to Ireland. The proposed travelers were her chief academic officer, the student life director, a counseling office secretary, three faculty members, a community member, a board member and spouse, and the student body president. The trip, paid through the college's general fund, was to build relationships with an Irish technical college to expand student exchange opportunities. A local travel agency, owned by a board member's neighbor, had provided a generous discount on hotels and airfare in return for being the district's sole travel agency.

Alice was concerned about the request and asked her chief academic officer for more information. He told her not to worry; the college had sponsored trips like this every year—one in the winter and one in the summer—for the last seven years. College employees took turns going, and the previous president had viewed the trip as a reward for hard work and dedication. He noted that at least five of the people scheduled for this year's travel had not yet taken their turn at an international trip. He assured Alice that she was welcome to join them and offered to place a call to the travel agent for her.

Although the opening story emphasizes a new president's dilemma surrounding a travel request, this chapter's primary audience is community college professionals at all levels of the institution. The travel incident is symptomatic of a larger ethical challenge facing the entire institution. Embedded in the case are multiple ethical questions. The incident we selected could as well have been about other collegewide issues such as athletics, grades, faculty credentials, or budget. We selected a travel example because several community colleges and community college systems have recently faced similar events. Using this case scenario as a springboard, we focus on the very real, often messy, and always complex issues of forging and maintaining an ethical culture within the institution. This endeavor begins with leaders and their willingness to reflect on their own professional ethical identity and their ability to facilitate the development of the institution's ethical identity. By "institutional ethical identity," we mean how the community college operates and views itself through an ethical lens. We agree with Wildes (1997) that "institutions can have a moral identity and conscience" (p. 415) and that this moral or ethical identity is communicated through the institution's mission and is the foundation of the community college's institutional ethics.

NEW DIRECTIONS FOR COMMUNITY COLLEGES • DOI: 10.1002/cc

Working through and deciding what you would do in the opening scenario depends as much on your place or "fit" within the institution (Harding, 2004; Schein, 2004; Geertz, 1995) as it does your own individual views, values, and ethics. The match or fit between the value sets of the individual, the subgroup or department, the institution, and the community in which the institution resides can be assessed and examined using the ethical identity framework elaborated on by Anderson, Harbour, and Davies (2007). This framework is based on the ethical acculturation model of Handelsman, Gottlieb, and Knapp (2005) and Berry's model of acculturation (Berry, 1980, 2003; Berry and Sam, 1997). We contend that many of the ethical issues in community colleges, although influenced by leaders and others, are beyond the ultimate control of just one or even several individuals. In reality, faculty, staff, and administrators join together in a web of relationships, processes, and obligations that create the institution's ethical identity. This ethical identity is communicated through the institution's mission and values and is the foundation of the community college's institutional ethics.

We began with an overview of the community college culture and the community college's challenges and complexities. Next, we discuss the concept of ethical acculturation and the tension that exists when individual ethics and values conflict with those of the institution. Finally, we propose ways for leaders and constituents to work together to build an institution's ethical identity through professional development opportunities, daily activities, and decision making. This praxis brings together the ethical identity of individuals and the ethical culture of subgroups to clarify the moral identity and conscience (Wildes, 1997) of the institution into the larger cultural and ethical context in which all exist (Woody, 2008; Anderson, Harbour, and Davies, 2007; Vaughan, 1992). We believe that having these strategies in place will help leaders and the campus community as a whole navigate the ethically complex and challenging issues faced on a daily basis, ultimately shaping the ethical identity of the institution.

Throughout this chapter, we use the terms *institution, organization*, and *college* interchangeably. Further, when we speak of employees and individuals, we assume that each member of the college belongs to one or more subgroups within the institution.

The Community College: Its Culture, Challenges, and Complexities

Regardless of size, age, history, or culture, most community colleges publicly articulate four primary values: open access, comprehensive mission, student success, and service to the community (Anderson, Harbour, and Davies, 2007; Hegeman, Davies, and Banning, 2007). These four values provide a focus and opportunity for individuals, subgroups, and institutions to develop shared understandings and common professional and institutional ethical identities. However, in today's community college, both the institution and its members are trying to balance a variety of issues (Dougherty, 2003), including changing student and employee demographics, pedagogical and curricular shifts, advances in technology, aging physical facilities, increased competition, multiple and conflicting opportunities, reliance on partnerships, mission drift, diminishing budgets, increased scrutiny and calls for accountability, and all the other realities of today's community college world (Cohen and Brawer, 2008).

In striving to meet the challenges, community college professionals find themselves trying to fulfill their social contract, provide good stewardship of the resources entrusted to them, and meet public expectations within that ethical framework (Vaughan, 1992). At the same time, community colleges are dealing with competing internal values and beliefs in a complex culture comprised of a variety of individuals and subgroups (Locke and Guglielmino, 2006; Baker and Associates, 1992).

Evaluating an organization's culture is complex (Schein, 2004). America's community colleges are multifaceted organizations filled with many different individuals and subgroups with sometimes conflicting beliefs and goals (Cohen and Brawer, 2008). Tracing the development of America's community colleges (Witt and others, 1994), we find that most have reached a stage of institutional maturity where institutional culture, values, and practices are deeply rooted in beliefs sometimes hard to dissect or change (Alfred, 2008). In addition, many community colleges have evolved from small, centralized, homogeneous organizations to highly complex ones relying increasingly on specialists and part-time employees (Alfred, 2008).

Within the institution, each subgroup has evolved its own subculture based on history, prior experiences, professional affiliations, and personal beliefs of members (Woody, 2008; Martin, 2002). The result is competing internal values and beliefs about what is best for the institution and its stakeholders. Having strategies to help the institution and its members handle the complexities and challenges in ways that honor ethical standards and boundaries is important and necessary.

Usually, the expectation for finding a way to "fix" these conflicts falls to the leader. The leader alone cannot manage these challenges; it takes the effort and will of all employees, that is, the development of a collective sense of institutional ethics. We believe that one way to meet the challenges is for individuals and subgroups within the institution to come together around common beliefs and values to forge a solid professional and institutional ethical identity clearly articulated through the college's vision, mission, values, and actions. This coming together would start with building an awareness of the organizational complexities and subcultures (Schein, 2004) as well as matching the cultural values of the community college with those of the individuals who work there.

Ethical Acculturation and the Community College Culture

Community colleges have their own culture and subcultures. Becoming part of these cultures is not an automatic experience; the adapting or acculturating process over a period of time develops an individual's professional ethical identity (Anderson, Harbour, and Davies, 2007; Handelsman, Gottlieb, and Knapp, 2005). The acculturation process involves two tasks: "cultural maintenance" and "contact and participation" (Berry and Sam, 1997, p. 296). For example, as professionals enter a community college as employees, they consciously or unconsciously consider what core values and personal ethics they'll maintain as they interact within the organization (cultural maintenance) as well as whether they will embrace or reject the institutional values and organizational ethics (contact and participation). The resolution of these two tasks manifests itself in one of four acculturation strategies: marginalization, separation, assimilation, and integration (Handelsman, Gottlieb, and Knapp, 2005). We briefly summarize these four strategies by returning to the opening scenario to illustrate how each strategy might look in practice. (We refer you to Anderson, Harbour, and Davies, 2007; Harbour, Anderson, and Davies, 2007; and Handelsman, Gottlieb, and Knapp, 2005, for a more in-depth discussion of ethical acculturation and professional ethical identity.)

> *Marginalization strategy (low in "maintenance" and low in "contact and participation").* Alice's first response was one of disbelief. She decided to contact the previous president to get his perspective on the situation. During the conversation, she realized that her predecessor had let the event happen year after year because he "saw no real problem with the travel" and hadn't been "called on the carpet" by anyone. Alice hung up the phone wondering what else she might uncover during her first year at the college.

The former president had sensed no problems and had not received a reprimand for allowing the travel; therefore, we might assume that he was operating from the marginalization strategy in this scenario. Individuals operating from this strategy are willing to follow policies or ethical guidelines out of convenience or to stay out of trouble. They have limited or few personal values that guide their ethical decision making. If there are ethical policies or processes in the organization, they have little interest in following them. In our opening scenario, it is very likely that Alice's predecessor demonstrated the marginalization strategy.

> *Separation strategy (high in "maintenance" and low in "contact and participation").* Alice took stock of her own sense of right and wrong in relationship to the travel request. Although there was a brief moment of self-doubt about her strong response to the request, she knew in her heart that this trip was

ethically problematic for many reasons. Even though the institution's values were in conflict with hers and she faced the discomfort of making an unpopular decision as the new president, she began to think about how she might address the issue as well as shift the culture.

Individuals who choose the separation strategy have a "well-developed ethical sense" (Handelsman, Gottlieb, and Knapp, 2005, p. 61). In our opening case, Alice is drawing on her own sense of right and wrong while questioning the values of the institution. In this particular scenario, the separation strategy makes good ethical sense. Alice's moral challenge will be to hold on to her core values even though the initial response by others will likely be disappointment, anger, and political posturing. As the leader, her job will be to articulate her ethical concerns clearly and without a judgmental attitude.

> *Assimilation strategy (low in "maintenance" and high in "contact and participation").* At one point, Alice was tempted just to go with the status quo, ignoring her own professional and personal values. She knew it would be easier to accept the chief academic officer's recommendation and began to wonder if she was the one whose standards didn't "fit" NSCC's culture. Was she overreacting?

Individuals who choose the assimilation strategy have overly identified with the organization or profession. They have cast aside their own core values of right and wrong without taking time to critically examine the organizational values and ethics (Anderson, Harbour, and Davies, 2007). In our opening scenario, it is possible that at one time, Alice's chief academic officer and even the previous president had concerns regarding the ethics of the international trip. But for various reasons, they decided to rationalize away the ethical concerns.

> *Integration Strategy (high in "maintenance" and high in "contact and participation").* Alice pondered her dilemma. If she put an immediate stop to the long-standing travel practice, she'd be signaling her ethical standards, but at what cost? How could she make the changes she knew were necessary? Alice reflected on what she knew about institutions with strong codes of ethics and practices supporting highly integrated ethical identity development. What was it about those places that provided a foundation for making wise choices individually and collectively?

When individuals can adapt to the organization's ethics and values while maintaining their personal code of ethics, there is a better match between person and profession. A cautionary point is how the integration strategy might manifest itself when the organization's ethical practices may be lacking or fall short. This is the situation for Alice at her new institution. Although there may be a tension between a professional's and the organization's sense of right and wrong, individuals seek to resolve the tension in a way that fosters even more integration between themselves and the profession or organization (Handelsman, Gottlieb, and Knapp, 2005). Alice is assessing the possibility of her own possibly flawed ethical thinking while considering how she might foster greater ethical sensitivity among her faculty and staff. This approach provides the best option for developing a professional ethical identity benefiting the individual and the institution (Anderson, Harbour, and Davies, 2007).

Acculturation Mismatch

The acculturation model proposed by Handelsman, Gottlieb, and Knapp (2005) is grounded in the assumption that the profession or professional organization espouses ethical standards that reach for the ethical ideal or are beneficent. In the opening scenario, Alice is facing an institutional practice that is ethically problematic, if not clearly unethical. Anderson, Harbour, and Davies (2007) suggest that leaders avoid the integration strategy when organizational values are lacking or corrupt. If we were ethical consultants to Alice, we would remind her that successful integration "requires that personal beliefs and college values be recognized as reasonable ideals" (Anderson, Harbour, and Davies, 2007, p. 66).

The opposite is possible as well: a new leader might bring personal values into an institution that should not be integrated into the organizational culture. For example, a new leader may have a self-serving perspective on the importance of service to the community. She may view the community as a means to an end rather than an equal entity in the community college mission. This attitude does not suggest an appropriate integration strategy.

Alice's dilemma illustrates just one of the many ethical challenges faced daily at community colleges across the country. We believe it is important for community college professionals to recognize instances of marginalization, separation, and assimilation as they continue to create better opportunities for themselves, their employees, and their institution to integrate ethical beliefs and values.

Creating Opportunities for Professional and Institutional Ethical Identity Development

As discussed in Anderson, Harbour, and Davies (2007), supporting an integration strategy for community college leaders respects one's personal ethics while focusing on the community college mission and contributing to the college's overall ethical identity or institutional ethics. Those authors recommend that community college leaders initiate collaborative collegewide dialogues, create and instill the institution's decrees of purpose, design operational guidelines, and support continual engagement activities, which we would suggest promotes multiple opportunities for advancing the institution's ethical identity. As part of the acculturation process, these activities help individuals assess and integrate their own personal ethics and professional identity with the college's ethical identity. Ultimately, these formal and informal activities should communicate clearly the institution's ethical identity to internal and external stakeholders.

Informal or formal institutionwide dialogues engage employees and help the leader focus on integrating the institution's ethical identity. Institutionwide dialogues also provide opportunities for the college's ethical identity development. By articulating clearly the institution's values while acknowledging the individual's personal ethics through continual employee engagement, leaders can promote an integration acculturation strategy. Other activities promoting ethical identity development include formalizing the institution's decree of purpose through mission, vision, and values statements.

Clarifying the Institution's Mission, Purpose, and Values. David (1989) defined a mission statement as "an enduring statement of purpose that distinguishes one organization from other similar enterprises, a mission statement is an organization's reason for being" (p. 90). Creating and defining the mission provides a common institutional direction. Hegeman, Davies, and Banning (2007) asserted that "clearly articulated mission statement messages tell internal and external stakeholders what the community college will do and, by implication, what it cannot (or will not) do" (p. 132). These authors concurred with the notion that the mission statement must dictate a strong sense of purpose and provide direction for employees' conduct. It should motivate and inspire employees to support the institution's ethical identity through a shared direction or vision.

When employees collectively design a vision statement, this creates a clear and vibrant declaration of what the institution wants to become. Imagining a stirring, captivating, and attractive future engages and motivates the institution. Vision statements inspire, describe the future, set out a specific goal, and drive action toward achieving the goal. By combining a proclaimed mission with an arousing vision and strong values, they can mold and provide guidance for the institution's ethical identity.

By integrating the institution's values, accepting the mission, embracing the vision, and promoting the shared values and beliefs, employees begin to understand the institution's ethical identity in four ways. First, shared values provide meaning for the mission's purpose and employees' conduct. Second, Campbell (1989) affirms that employees work harder when they believe in what they are doing and trust the institution. Third, Bart (1997) proposes that employees who do not embrace the values either quit or are encouraged to leave due to the mismatch with the institution's identity. Finally, strong values guide daily decision making. Mission, vision, and values provide three key cornerstones communicating the institution's ethical identity to all stakeholders. Intentionally displaying the mission, vision, and values statements throughout the institution provide ongoing reminders of the organization's guiding principles. Designing operational guidelines such as a code of ethics provides another formal product delineating the institution's ethical identity.

Developing a Code of Ethics. A code of ethics serves as a central guide upon which to make daily decisions. The American Association of Community Colleges' *Recommended Code of Ethics for Chief Executive Officers of Community Colleges* (2005) addresses standards for personal conduct and institutional leadership for CEOs. These standards point to core values; responsibilities to board members, administration, faculty, and staff; responsibilities to students; responsibilities to other educational institutions; responsibilities to business, civic groups, and the community at large; and they conclude with a listing of the chief executive officers' rights. Davis (2008) describes an intentional, collaborative process for developing an institutional code of ethics. A code of ethics "is meant to clarify an organization's mission, values, and principles, linking them with standards of professional conduct" (Ethics Resource Center, 2009).

We believe that the code of ethics should reflect the institution's ethical identity. Past experiences and collective understanding of right and wrong influence the code's content. New employees should receive the code so that they become familiar with the institution's philosophy, ethics, values, and core principles. College employees' annual code review and subsequent approval declare its viability. Infusing the code's content into the college culture promotes ongoing integration encompassing daily practices. The code's use as an accountability tool reinforces the acculturation of the institution's ethical identity. Finally, the code's principles serve as a basis for daily collegewide engagement activities.

It is nearly impossible to create a code of ethics without also developing and adhering to an institutional philosophy. Many philosophical beliefs evolve through institutional activities supported by financial commitment and continual collaborative collegewide participation. Additional philosophical tenets should outline processes for acknowledging disagreements, resolving conflict, and promoting consensus building. The institution can assess its philosophical stance and strive for continuous improvement by measuring actions and decisions against its ethical code.

Informal and formal activities provide continual opportunities for developing and infusing the mission, vision, and values and integrating the institution's philosophy. Daily decision making using the code of conduct as an accountability standard underscores the institution's ethical identity. Informal activities reflecting its standards may be as simple as modeling behaviors through daily oral and written communications ranging from casual hallway conversations to e-mails. Formal activities encouraging collaborative institutionwide dialogues may include more complex activities, such as collegewide facilitated conversations, accreditation processes, budget development, and strategic planning initiatives. The code should continue to serve as an authority for ethical decision making even when more challenging issues arise, as when making difficult financial decisions during challenging economic times. Additional activities that would benefit from the influence of the code include employee orientation, leadership academies, mentoring programs, and professional development seminars. Encouraging celebrations and supporting traditions uphold the cultural norms and promote the institution's ethical identity while providing employees with opportunities for acculturation.

> Alice called the chancellor to discuss her concerns. She explained why she believed NSCC's past practices would not meet the "newspaper test" and sought his advice. Together they agreed that the December trip could proceed as planned, but attendees needed to provide detailed reports on outcomes and results. The chancellor agreed that he had some work to do with the governing board. Furthermore, he liked Alice's recommendations to conduct collegewide conversations regarding the mission, vision, values, and institutional philosophy and to develop a district code of ethics from which NSCC could develop its own.

Final Thoughts

We acknowledge and celebrate the complexities of today's community colleges and agree with other authors that promoting and facilitating integration strategies for community college leaders could be an onerous task (Anderson, Harbour, and Davies, 2007; Harbour, Anderson, and Davies, 2007). We recognize the existence of three very different and sometimes contradictory entities within our organizations: individual employees, various subgroups, and the institution as a whole. A reciprocal process is necessary in order to encourage multiple voices as we build an institutional ethical identity. Campus leaders will need to respect the values of subgroups and the values and experiences of new employees who make up these subgroups; simultaneously, the campus community as a whole will need to work with the leaders to help them harmonize their core values with the foundational principles of community colleges (Anderson, Harbour, and Davies, 2007).

By using a complex scenario and offering reflective vignettes that expand the scenario, we have briefly reviewed the four acculturation strategies. In addition, we have provided an opportunity for readers to consider their own (and their institution's) ethical acculturation status. We believe it is critical for individuals to find ways to identify and integrate their respective perspectives into a collective professional and institutional ethical identity, and we offer practical suggestions for doing so.

NEW DIRECTIONS FOR COMMUNITY COLLEGES • DOI: 10.1002/cc

Activities that contribute to the institution's professional ethical identity development include professional development opportunities focusing on the institution's cultural identity; defining the institution's purpose through mission, vision, and value statements; collaboratively creating a code of ethics; providing norms for leadership actions; and embracing collegewide engagement activities. These support institutional decision making, especially when dealing with complex ethical issues. The institution's publicly proclaimed ethical identity provides a benchmark for employees to use in developing their own personal and professional ethical identities and offers opportunities for all to acculturate appropriately.

Finally, regardless of our role in the community college, we can never forget our fundamental reason for being. For many students, "the choice is not between the community college and a senior residential institution; it is between the community college and nothing" (Cohen and Brawer, 2008, p. 58). Our responsibility as community college professionals is to ensure that our professional and institutional ethical identity is strong and integrated with our mission so that we can face today's challenges and continue to provide access and opportunity to our students and our communities.

Guiding Questions

1. Which ethical acculturation strategy is dominant in your institution?
2. Reflect on a time in your life when you have felt as if you (and your values) did not "fit" within an organization. Which of the ethical acculturation strategies did you use? What would you do differently today? What did you do well then?
3. Reflect on individuals and organizations with which you have some familiarity. Describe an example of each of the ethical acculturation strategies (marginalization, separation, assimilation, and integration) you have observed. What insights and suggestions can you offer for dealing with each situation?
4. What components would you include in your institution's code of ethics? What processes would you use to elicit buy-in and participation? What processes would not work in your current culture or climate? Why?
5. Design a process for continual improvement by measuring actions and decisions against your institution's ethical code. What assessment strategies could you use to ensure continual improvement? How would you engage the institution in the process?

References

Alfred, R. L. *Governance in Strategic Context*. New Directions for Community Colleges, no. 141. San Francisco: Jossey-Bass, 2008.

American Association of Community Colleges. *Recommended Code of Ethics for Chief Executive Officers of Community Colleges*. 2005. [http://www.aacc.nche.edu]. Nov. 2, 2008.

Anderson, S. K., Harbour, C. P., and Davies, T. G. "Professional Ethical Identity Development and Community College Leadership." In D. A. Hellmich (ed.), *Ethical Leadership in the Community College: Bridging Theory and Daily Practice*. Bolton, Mass.: Anker, 2007.

Baker, G. A., III, and Associates. *Cultural Leadership: Inside America's Community Colleges*. Washington, D.C.: Community College Press, 1992.

Bart, C. K. "Sex, Lies, and Mission Statements." *Business Horizons*, 1997, *40*, 9–19.

Berry, J. W. "Acculturation as Varieties of Adaptation." In A. M. Padilla (ed.), *Acculturation: Theory, Models, and Some New Findings*. Boulder, Colo.: Westview, 1980.

Berry, J. W. "Conceptual Approaches to Acculturation." In K. M. Chun, P. B. Organista, and G. Marin (eds.), *Acculturation: Advances in Theory, Measurement, and Applied Research*. Washington, DC: American Psychological Association, 2003.

Berry, J. W., and Sam, D. L. "Acculturation and Adaptation." In J. W. Berry, M. H. Segall, and C. Kagitcibasi (eds.), *Handbook of Cross-Cultural Psychology, Vol. 3: Social Behavior and Applications* (2nd ed.). Boston: Allyn & Bacon, 1997.

Campbell, A. "Does Your Organization Need a Mission?" *Leadership and Organization Development Journal*, 1989, *10*, 3–9.

Cohen, A. M. and Brawer, F. B. *The American Community College* (5th ed.). San Francisco: Jossey-Bass, 2008.

David, F. R. "How Companies Define Their Mission." *Long Range Planning*, 1989, *22*, 90–97.

Davis, M. "Thinking Through the Issues in a Code of Ethics." In D. G. Terkla (ed.), *Institutional Research: More Than Just Data*. New Directions for Higher Education, no. 141. San Francisco: Jossey-Bass, 2008.

Dougherty, K. "The Community College: The Origins, Impacts, and Futures of a Contradictory Institution." In J. Ballantine and J. Spade (eds.), *Schools and Society*. Belmont, Calif.: Wadsworth, 2003.

Ethics Resource Center. "Why Have a Code of Conduct?" [http://www.ethics.org/resource/why-have-code-conduct]. Jan. 24, 2009.

Geertz, C. *After the Fact: Two Countries, Four Decades, One Anthropologist*. Cambridge, Mass.: Harvard University Press, 1995.

Handelsman, M. M., Gottlieb, M. C., and Knapp, S. "Training Ethical Psychologists: An Acculturation Model." *Professional Psychology: Research and Practice*, 2005, *36*, 59–65.

Harbour, C. P., Anderson, S. K., and Davies, T. G. "The Consequences of Compromised Ethical Identity Development in Community College Leadership." In D. A. Hellmich (ed.), *Ethical Leadership in the Community College: Bridging Theory and Daily Practice*. Bolton, Mass.: Anker, 2007.

Harding, S. "Introduction: Standpoint Theory as a Site of Political, Philosophic, and Scientific Debate." In S. Harding (ed.), *The Feminist Standpoint Theory Reader: Intellectual and Political Controversies*. New York: Routledge, 2004.

Hegeman, D. L., Davies, T. G., and Banning, J. H. "Community Colleges' Use of the Web to Communicate Their Mission: Slights of Commission and Omission." *Community College Journal of Research and Practice*, 2007, *31*, 129–147.

Locke, M. G., and Guglielmino, L. "The Influence of Subcultures on Planned Change in a Community College." *Community College Review*, 2006, *34*, 108–127.

Martin, J. *Organizational Culture: Mapping the Terrain*. London: Sage, 2002.

Schein, E. H. *Organizational Culture and Leadership* (3rd ed.). San Francisco: Jossey-Bass, 2004.

Vaughan, G. B. (ed.). *Dilemmas of Leadership: Decision Making and Ethics in the Community College*. San Francisco: Jossey-Bass, 1992.

Wildes, K. W. "Institutional Identity, Integrity, and Conscience." *Kennedy Institute of Ethics Journal*, 1997, 7(41), 413–419.

Witt, A. A., Wattenbarger, J. L., Gollattscheck, J. F., and Suppiger, J. E. *America's Community Colleges: The First Century*. Washington, D.C.: Community College Press, 1994.

Woody, W. D. "Learning from the codes of the academic disciplines." In S. L. Moore (ed.), *Practical Approaches to Ethics for Colleges and Universities*. New Directions for Higher Education, no. 142. San Francisco: Jossey-Bass, 2008.

SHARON K. ANDERSON, associate professor, is the director of Graduate Programs in the School of Education at Colorado State University.

LINDA LUJAN is interim president of Chandler-Gilbert Community College, one of ten colleges and two skill centers In the Maricopa Community College District in Phoenix, Arizona.

DIANE L. HEGEMAN is vice president of instruction at Arapahoe Community College in Littleton, Colorado.

NEW DIRECTIONS FOR COMMUNITY COLLEGES • DOI: 10.1002/cc

3

*Ethical dilemmas at the community college often pose
a choice between options equally grounded in the core
values of the institution. These dilemmas often emerge
from disputes that are complex, dynamic, and politically
volatile. We review the development of one such dispute to
show how our understanding of institutional core
values is often only clarified through reflection and
consultation with appropriate advisors, authorities,
and constituencies.*

Ethical Dimensions of the Open-Door Admissions Policy

William G. Ingram, Sharon E. Morrissey

In the words of Rushworth Kidder, the "really tough choices . . . don't center upon right versus wrong. They involve right versus right. They are genuine dilemmas precisely because each side is firmly rooted in one of our basic, core values" (2006, p. 18). As in other leadership settings, the ethical challenges facing community college presidents can be framed as deciding among competing rights. Excellent examples of such competing rights can be found in the dilemmas that arise in the application of a core value of the community college mission: the philosophy of open access and the open-door admissions policy.

In this chapter, we offer the perspective of two community college presidents regarding a specific dilemma of institutional ethics that concerns the philosophy of open access and the open-door admissions policy. Our purpose is to explicate this dilemma in the following manner. First, we discuss the assumptions underlying the philosophy of open access and the open-door admissions policy. Second, we examine a specific instance where this philosophy and policy were implicated in a debate concerning the proper role of public community colleges in serving undocumented adult students. Third, after describing this debate and noting its twists and turns, we conclude by explaining how the true strength of core values like the philosophy of open access is sometimes best appreciated when tested in controversies that directly affect the operation of community colleges.

Defenders of the community college open-access philosophy argue that it is a necessary condition for realizing access to education for all adults (Vaughan, 1985). And access to education for all adults is needed if the

31

NEW DIRECTIONS FOR COMMUNITY COLLEGES, no. 148, Winter 2009 © 2009 Wiley Periodicals, Inc.
Published online in Wiley InterScience (www.interscience.wiley.com) • DOI: 10.1002/cc.384

American dream is to become a genuine opportunity for everyone. The connection between the American dream and a specific component of the open-access philosophy, that is, the open-door admissions policy, was described nearly half a century ago by early writers about two-year colleges. Medsker (1960) noted that the educational opportunities provided by two-year colleges through the open-door admissions policy reflected the nation's commitment to offering a pathway enabling everyone to realize the American desire to move up from one social class to the next. Yet the open-door admissions policy did more than provide access to social and economic well-being. As Roueche and Baker (1987) observed, the success of the American style of democratic government depends heavily on the existence of a well-informed populace. Accordingly, community college scholars have recognized the critical, albeit implicit, link between the open-access philosophy, the open-door admissions policy, and the promotion of American democracy. Roueche and Baker identified three developments in the history of American education as central to the creation of this well-informed citizenry: (1) the establishment of "common schools" in the first half of the nineteenth century, (2) the development of land-grant colleges in the second half of that century, and (3) the creation of the junior college at the turn of the twentieth century.

Thus the philosophy of open access and, more specifically, the open-door admissions policy is a necessary predicate to the community college's role of providing access to opportunity through education. If education is necessary for individuals to improve themselves socially and economically and to fully participate in democratic institutions, universal access to that education is required.

The open-door admissions policy is further predicated on a fundamental assumption about the student's capacity to benefit from the educational experience. Durham Technical Community College, for example, has adopted the philosophy of a "learning institution" and operates on the assumption, suggested by community college President Sanford Shugart (2004), that virtually all students have the capacity for success in their academic or technical pursuits. That assumption can be restated as this: under the proper conditions, any student can learn anything.

The role of the learning college, therefore, is to establish those conditions that best facilitate learning. In our careers as practitioners, we have found that a student's failure to learn is most often the result of poor preparation and skills deficits and not an innate ability to learn. This assumption forms an essential part of the justification for developmental education programs. That is, community college practitioners believe that with an opportunity to remediate, the vast majority of students can solidify their skills in English composition, reading, and mathematics and move on to more specialized instruction in areas that will lead to employment or transfer to four-year colleges and universities.

Another assumption implicit in the open-door admissions policy is that students have a "right to fail." In our view, in voluntary adult education settings, the right to fail is a consequence of the American commitment to freedom of choice in deciding how to lead one's life and determining one's destiny. The individual, with the freedom to choose to enroll in college and, once admitted, to invest sufficient time and effort toward success is simply exercising the right to take on the risk of failure.

The assumptions associated with the open-door admissions policy, however, can be challenged on several fronts. For example, the assertion that "under the proper conditions, anybody can learn anything" is difficult to prove. Individuals with diminished mental capacity due to brain injury, for example, are clearly incapable of learning certain things. "Ability to benefit" assessments are routinely used by community colleges to verify a capacity for academic success for students who lack a high school diploma or equivalent. Individuals who do not demonstrate this ability to benefit are not eligible for federal financial aid programs. The argument for assessing a student's ability to benefit from college admission is based on the expectation that public resources be used efficiently. Since financial aid dollars are finite, so the argument goes, they should not be spent to support a student who cannot benefit from admission.

This argument is extended further with the understanding that student learning ability exists on a continuum. The resources an institution must use to provide effective educational programs and services vary, depending on students' abilities. Put another way, the institution's capacity for providing the proper conditions for effective learning is dependent on resources, and there is the expectation that institutions will use their resources efficiently. Dollars spent on remedial or developmental programs are dollars not available for technical or transfer programs. Recognizing this, some states (including Massachusetts, New York, and Texas) limit state subsidies for remediation and delivery of developmental studies courses (Bastedo and Gumport, 2003). In effect, the efficient use of state resources to produce well-prepared technicians and transfer students competes with the ideal of the open-door admissions policy and the attendant belief that all students can learn.

To a lesser degree, this conflict between open-door admissions and efficient use of resources is found in policies regarding participation in allied health programs. In North Carolina, for example, a college's ability to offer the associate degree in nursing depends on approval by the state's board of nursing. Among the factors the state board considers in granting approval is the passing rate of a college's graduates on the national licensing examination. Thus to obtain approval from the state board of nursing, colleges frequently require students to demonstrate academic ability or achievement that goes beyond documentation of high school graduation.

Still, North Carolina has a long history of deep commitment to open access and the open-door admissions policy. Dallas Herring, generally considered the father of the North Carolina Community College System, articulated in 1963 the open-access philosophy for community college enrollments:

> The only valid philosophy . . . is the philosophy of total education; a belief in
> the incomparable worth of all human beings, whose claims upon the state are
> equal before the law and equal before the bar of public opinion; whose tal-
> ents (however great or however limited or however different from the tradi-
> tional) the state needs and must develop to the fullest possible degree. That
> is why the [community colleges'] doors must never be closed to anyone of
> suitable age who can learn what they teach [Wiggs, 1989, p. 13].

In addition to ethical challenges related to open-door admissions, capacity to succeed, and efficient use of public resources, a new politically fraught admissions issue has recently emerged in North Carolina that directly bears on the philosophical commitment to open access and the open-door admissions policy: the question as to whether undocumented immigrants should be allowed to enroll in the state's community colleges.

A January 2005 policy brief reported on the actions taken by five states in providing access to education programs for undocumented students (Biswas, 2005). North Carolina is one of five states included in the report, along with Florida, New Mexico, Texas, and Virginia. Each of these states has large or rapidly growing immigrant populations. The policy brief iden-tified two approaches taken by policymakers in these states: "(a) improving opportunity for undocumented students in higher education; and (b) dis-couraging access to higher education in favor of protecting citizens and tax-payers in a era of fiscal challenges" (p. 3).

North Carolina's community colleges have spent the past several years on a roller-coaster ride concerning the admission of undocumented immigrants. For example, in 2001, the general counsel for the North Carolina Community College System (NCCCS) issued "guidance to college administrators concern-ing admission or enrollment of undocumented or illegal aliens in programs or courses at community colleges" (Hines, 2001, p. 1). College administrators were advised not to enroll undocumented students in curriculum programs unless they were high school students who were taking college classes under the concurrent enrollment policy. The general counsel's advisory was not bind-ing on local boards of trustees, and by 2005, several colleges were admitting undocumented immigrants based on the open-door admissions policy adopted by the state board of the NCCCS and the authority granted to local boards of trustees by the North Carolina General Statutes (1979) to apply the requirements and standards for determining the proper admission of students.

As the immigrant population grew in North Carolina and as more and more undocumented students graduated from the state's high schools, ques-tions about their admission to community colleges continued to be raised. In November 2007, the general counsel to the NCCCS changed its earlier position on this issue and issued "New Guidance on the Admission of Undocumented Individuals" (Sullivan, 2007). The memorandum cited the open-door admissions policy and advised colleges to adopt local policies

NEW DIRECTIONS FOR COMMUNITY COLLEGES • DOI: 10.1002/cc

regarding the admission of undocumented students to curriculum programs at the out-of-state tuition rate. Approximately half of the fifty-eight community colleges in the state adopted policies allowing admission of undocumented students. However, because undocumented students were required to pay out-of-state tuition, only 112 out of 272,244 curriculum students enrolled in 2006–07 were identified as undocumented (North Carolina State Board of Community Colleges, 2008a).

In May 2008, the North Carolina attorney general entered the debate and released an advisory letter notifying community colleges that the practice of admitting undocumented students may be in conflict with federal immigration law and recommending that community colleges return to the 2001 practice of restricting admission of undocumented students to curriculum programs (North Carolina State Board of Community Colleges, 2008a). On May 13, 2008, the general counsel to the NCCCS issued another advisory superseding the November 2007 memorandum and instructed community colleges to cease admitting undocumented individuals to curriculum programs, except those who are concurrently enrolled high school students (Martin, 2008). The general counsel also requested formal clarification about federal restrictions from the U.S. Department of Homeland Security.

In July 2008, the Department of Homeland Security notified the North Carolina attorney general's office that federal immigration law does not restrict the admission of undocumented students into higher education institutions as long as no financial aid assistance is provided (Pendergraph, 2008). In response, the North Carolina attorney general advised the state board of the NCCCS to develop policies for admission of undocumented immigrants (Kelly, 2008). In addition, the attorney general cited the federal requirement that any state policy concerning immigration status must use federal immigration standards in determining which applicants are undocumented aliens (Kelly, 2008).

The state board of the NCCCS is presently conducting a study of the issues surrounding the admission of undocumented students to North Carolina community colleges (North Carolina State Board of Community Colleges, 2008b). While many facets of this discussion relate to federal laws and state board policy, the debate raises two ethical questions for community college leaders: Should colleges allocate scarce resources to train individuals who cannot legally enter the workforce at the expense of those who can? And will denying access to undocumented immigrants change the open-door mission of the North Carolina Community College System? We address these two questions in the order posed.

While some states have restricted the enrollment of undocumented students, others have established admission policies that provide in-state tuition and state financial aid for undocumented students (Biswas, 2005). Critics of such policies argue that these practices place additional fiscal burdens on community colleges with limited resources, are unfair to resident taxpaying citizens, and appear to reward illegal behaviors. However, many of the undocumented students in our public schools were brought into the United States as minors and have never returned to their homeland. As these students graduate from high school and seek higher education in North Carolina's community colleges, state policymakers must ask what their future prospects will be. If they gain admission to and graduate from higher education institutions, will these undocumented immigrants then face federal employment laws prohibiting them from gaining legal employment in the United States?

The pending admission decision may affect the NCCCS's long-standing open-door mission. Its mission statement reads, in part, "The mission of the North Carolina Community College System is to open the door to high-quality, accessible educational opportunities that minimize barriers to post-secondary education, maximize student success, develop a globally and multi-culturally competent workforce, and improve the lives and well-being of individuals" (North Carolina State Board of Community Colleges, 2009).

In 1963, when Herring advocated for a philosophy of open access, the ethical issue of whether or not to subsidize college education for undocumented immigrants had not been raised.

There are many arguments for and against open access for all of the people who reside in our communities. The state board's decision about admission of undocumented immigrants is one of those "really tough choices" described by Kidder (2006) that exemplifies many modern ethical dilemmas where the choice is between two options both grounded in our core values. Our purpose in highlighting this issue of institutional ethics is twofold.

First, our discussion reveals how state community college administrators and local college officials may be challenged by dynamic and complex ethical issues that are politically volatile in the community. In these circumstances, both state administrators and local college officials are wise to consult with their governing boards, senior staff, community constituencies, and legal counsel. Open communication and informed discussion in campus settings that seek to educate and not legislate offer the potential for learning and informed decision making about procedures that are consistent with policies established by state and local governing authorities.

Second, our experience in North Carolina with this issue reaffirms to us that institutional missions and, in particular, the commitment to open access and the open-door admissions policy are from time to time tested on campus, in the media, and in the community. In our case, we view this process as a reflection that the open-access philosophy and the open-door admissions policy remain important and relevant to how community colleges should be serving their communities. The philosophy and policy are based on ideals that continue to be essential to the growth and prosperity of our students, our communities, and our institutions. To be sure, this philosophy and its attendant policy may lead us into debates that can be contentious, but the North Carolina example reminds us that the value of our ideals is often only clear in the long run—that is, when we have seen how competing rights may be resolved and then ordered in a manner that best serves our students and our publics.

Guiding Questions

1. Is your institution permitted to enroll resident undocumented adults at in-state or in-district tuition rates? If so, is this authority granted by the state legislature, a state agency, a state governing or coordinating board, or a local governing board?
2. Has your institution reflected on the ethical issues involved in serving undocumented adults? Has this discussion been facilitated or conducted in an organized panel or forum?
3. How do your faculty and staff reflect on the meaning of the open-access philosophy and the open-door admissions policy? What priority do they place on this philosophy and this policy with respect to other institutional values?

References

Bastedo, M. N., and Gumport, P. J. "Access to What? Mission Differentiation and Academic Stratification in U.S. Public Higher Education." *Higher Education*, 2003, *43*, 341–359.

Biswas, R. R. *Access to Community College for Undocumented Immigrants: A Guide for State Policymakers.* Boston: Jobs for the Future, 2005.

Hines, C. T. "Admission or Enrollment of Undocumented or Illegal Aliens." *North Carolina Community College System Numbered Memorandum, CC01–271,* 2001.

Kelly, J. B. "Letter from North Carolina Department of Justice, Raleigh, to Ms. Shante Martin, General Counsel, North Carolina Community College System." July 24, 2008.

Kidder, R. *How Good People Make Tough Choices: Resolving the Dilemmas of Ethical Living.* New York: HarperCollins, 2006.

Martin, Q. S. "Unrestricted Admission of Undocumented or Illegal Immigrants." *North Carolina Community College System Numbered Memorandum, CC08–114,* May 13, 2008.

Medsker, L. *The Junior College: Progress and Prospect.* New York: McGraw-Hill, 1960.

North Carolina General Statutes. "Powers and Duties of Trustees." Ch. 115D-20 (4), 1979.

North Carolina State Board of Community Colleges. "Admission of Undocumented Individuals to N.C. Community College Curriculum Programs." Briefing paper presented to State Board of Community Colleges, Aug. 15, 2008a.

North Carolina State Board of Community Colleges. "Minutes of Board Meeting." Aug. 15, 2008b.

North Carolina State Board of Community Colleges. "System Mission." [http://www.nccommunitycolleges.edu/External_Affairs/system_mission.htm]. Aug. 13, 2009.

Pendergraph, J. "Letter from U.S. Department of Homeland Security Immigration and Customs Enforcement, Washington, D.C., to Mr. Thomas J. Ziko, Special Deputy Attorney General, North Carolina Department of Justice, Raleigh, N.C." July 9, 2008.

Roueche, J. E., and Baker, G. A. *Access and Excellence: The Open-Door College.* Washington, D.C.: Community College Press, 1987.

Shugart, S. C. Remarks delivered to the conference of the North Carolina Community College Instructional Administrators' Association at Wrightsville Beach, N.C., Mar. 31, 2004.

Sullivan, D. "New Guidance on the Admission of Undocumented Individuals." *North Carolina Community College System Numbered Memorandum, CC07–275*, 2007.

Vaughan, G. B. "Maintaining Open Access and Comprehensiveness." In D. Puyear (ed.), *Maintaining Institutional Integrity*. New Directions for Community Colleges, no. 52. San Francisco: Jossey-Bass, 1985.

Wiggs, J. L. *The Community College System in North Carolina: A Silver Anniversary History, 1963–1988*. Raleigh: North Carolina State Board of Community Colleges, 1989.

WILLIAM G. INGRAM *is president of Durham Technical Community College in Durham, North Carolina.*

SHARON E. MORRISSEY *is president of Richmond Community College in Hamlet, North Carolina.*

NEW DIRECTIONS FOR COMMUNITY COLLEGES • DOI: 10.1002/cc

This chapter raises awareness about potential approaches to institutional decision making in community colleges that embody diversity-affirming ethics and a critical epistemological orientation that promotes social justice.

Diversity-Affirming Ethics and Critical Epistemology: Institutional Decision Making in Community Colleges

Antonette Aragon, Edward J. Brantmeier

Arguably, central to the mission of most community colleges is the ideal of access to education in a commitment to American democracy and "justice for all." Premised on the principles of open access, a comprehensive mission, and service to the community (Bragg, 2001), community colleges make access possible and affordable for those who would otherwise remain marginalized from higher education because of life circumstances; lack of social, capital, or economic capital; societal constraints; or systemic or institutional barriers to social and economic mobility. Arguably, community colleges hold the potential for being the social institutions most capable of leveling and transforming the playing field for the historically marginalized; these colleges can and often do serve as catalysts for social change. We believe that community colleges have the potential to be vanguards for social justice, understood here as fair and just institutional or structural arrangements and personal, social, and professional relationships that provide access, opportunity, and inclusion of historically marginalized or otherwise oppressed individuals or groups of people. However, well-intentioned ideals must contend with the challenges of the everyday realities of institutions, their leaders, and the students who come through their doors. The principle of open access, the intentions of a comprehensive mission, and service to the community can fall short amid the everyday realities and constraints of doing business in community colleges.

The purpose of this chapter is to continue and potentially expand the conversation about how a diversity-affirming ethical orientation and an understanding of critical epistemology might guide institutional decision making in community colleges in the direction of social justice. Both of us are multicultural educators who hope to bring theory and practice in K–12 schooling and teacher education into dialogue with the possibilities and the constraints of community colleges as institutions for social change. The chapter begins with a conceptual overview of the terms *diversity ethics* and *critical epistemology* and then discusses how these concepts might be practically used to think through the complexities of curriculum and instruction as well as institutional access and opportunity. Our overall intention is to add opportunities for discourse on ethics in decision making by community college practitioners and multicultural educators in general.

Philosophical and Conceptual Overview

The study of ethics, related to the Greek words *ethos* and *character*, involve considerations of right versus wrong in decision making, as well as relative and universal standards of right and wrong. Among the questions stemming from ethical considerations in decision making: What are the criteria for determining rightness and wrongness? What values ought to guide decisions? Who will benefit from decisions? And what will the impact be for certain groups, individuals, the institution, or society as a whole?

Diversity Ethics. A diversity-affirming ethical orientation prescriptively promotes diversity in decision making. Premised on the principle of diversity affirmation or the notion that difference and multiplicity are positive, good, and beneficial to the institution, society, humanity, and the planet, diversity ethics supports a pluralistic perspective and reality. In this conception, differences along the lines of race or ethnicity, gender, class, religion, language, sexual orientation, ability, or nonconformity are considered positive attributes and assets to the functioning of institutions and society. Diversity in thought, emotion, and action are valued as well. Diversity in representation and inclusive practices emerge as selective advantages for survival and flourish amid social, political, economic, and environmental change. Diversity integration and inclusive practices also foster a reconciliation process toward social justice, a process that aims to overcome the legacy of past power differentials and related privileges associated with race, gender, and class in the United States. A diversity ethic steeped in social justice assumes that the playing field was never level for all because of institutional, societal, and structural inequities. A new field altogether needs to be built via social reconstruction (Sleeter and Grant, 1999), and educational institutions are one place to begin the process.

The contested ethical terrain of community college decision making ranges from ethical decisions about promoting access and opportunity, providing a comprehensive curriculum, implementing a budget, prioritizing

New Directions for Community Colleges • DOI: 10.1002/cc

and responding to community needs, administering financial aid, policing academic honesty, and implementing institutional policies regarding college property, technology use, and communal and business partnerships (Wallin, 2007; Davis, 2007). If these decisions were to be guided by a diversity ethic, considerations of rightness and wrongness in the decision-making process would be guided by the principle that diversity is positive, advantageous, and helpful to individuals, institutions, and society. A hierarchical framework that places diversity near the top might govern other valuations in the decision-making process. For example, diversity over sameness might supersede decisions in the curriculum development and hiring processes. Rather than conformity, uniformity, or similarity to the status quo, diversity might be embraced as positive and collectively beneficial for institutional flourishing and change.

Critical Epistemology. Within the framework of diversity-affirming ethics, community colleges might value curricular implications that foster student growth through an informed multilayered knowledge base while also preparing students for social mobility within workforce and civic participation. What and how knowledge is taught and valued affects social memory; this in turn reinforces a certain version of history that influences present-day public policy, legislation, and rules governing civic life (Howard, 2006). The telling of history perpetuates power differentials among groups in society, and the construction of knowledge may be relegated to the underpinnings of epistemological tenets.

Epistemology, or the theory of knowledge, focuses on central questions, including, "the origin of knowledge; the place of experience in generating knowledge, and the place of reason in doing so; the relationship between knowledge and certainty and between knowledge and the impossibility of error; the possibility of universal skepticism; and the changing forms of knowledge that arise from new conceptualizations of the world. All of these issues link with other central concerns of philosophy such as the nature of truth and the nature of experience and meaning" (Blackburn, 1994, p. 123).

Critical epistemology can be understood as an approach to understanding the origin, nature, and process of knowledge construction that takes into account unequal power dynamics inherent amid oppressive conditions. Carspecken (1996) maintains that "criticalists find contemporary society to be unfair, unequal, and both subtly and overtly oppressive for many people. We do not like it, and we want to change it" (p. 7). A critical epistemological approach, focused on understanding the origin, nature, and process of knowledge construction, involves questioning dominant and subordinate relationships between and among groups and individuals in society, as well as questioning the knowledge construction processes that enable continuation of oppressive, unjust conditions.

Education in the community college setting is concerned with the transmission of knowledge that allows students to think critically while developing skills that prepare them for the workforce and advancement in their careers. Community colleges also provide courses for self-improvement and further educational pursuits. Such knowledge acquisition processes may foster curiosity to question the nature of experience and meaning.

It is through the experience of meaning that students may desire to continue their education in the community college setting. The instructors of community colleges must transmit knowledge via current curricula that provide relevant skills for twenty-first-century readiness. Yet throughout American higher education, the epistemological rootedness of knowledge that is transferred to students is typically geared toward a Eurocentric worldview. Reinforcement of a Eurocentric worldview limits the impacts of the operational practices in community colleges because it caters to members of the dominant group in the United States and neglects inclusion of the voices of people of color.

An epistemological perspective is transferred to students both consciously and unconsciously. It is transferred through history, policies, educational practices, curricula, and curricular theories of courses. The infrastructure of American society is based on the Western, Eurocentric canon (Banks, 2001). European Americans are benefiting from systems of institutions that are made by them and for them. For example, property rights, and therefore rights to participate in the political process, were originally given only to white males. That legacy of economic power and racial privilege has translated into whiteness as a form of cultural and economic currency in the broader U.S. society (Ladson-Billings and Tate, 1995). Given that certain types of cultural currency are valued more than others in mainstream institutions, it is important to examine how the monocultural epistemological nature of the curriculum affects students' awareness and knowledge paradigms today.

Dominant American cultural values are built on a Eurocentric epistemology, which itself is based on "a strong faith in competitive, hierarchical capitalism (meritocracy), possessive individualism (consumerism), mechanistic science and technicist social policy, a utilitarian and exploitive relationship to the natural world, a mythological sense of national identity, and a moralistic-behaviorist image of the human being" (Akintunde, 2006, p. 36). Therefore, students outside of the western Eurocentric perspective are often excluded from institutional mobility because they experience significant institutional barriers. They either are unaware of or resist different forms of cultural capital valued by members of the culture of power (Delpit, 1988). In turn, the cultural capital of people of color is devalued and viewed as a deficit rather than as a potential asset for institutional and societal flourishing. Oppressive conditions are reinforced through systems of dominance (Howard, 2006).

An example of how race has been constructed will further clarify how institutions perpetuate a Eurocentric epistemology. The examination of race was socially constructed as a cultural and political creation that promoted colonial expansion, domination, and control, and it is now a socially acceptable category within the study of human diversity. Historically, the concept of race also served to create emotional and psychological distance between Europeans and other visually different peoples (Akintunde, 1999). A further analysis of historical construction of race also supports the assertion that race was constructed by Europeans to establish "whiteness" as "a cultural, systemic, epistemological privileged, and superior polemic" (p. 3). As racial categorization became an accepted means of classification, a hierarchical system was adopted to separate groups of people into "superior" (white) versus "inferior" (nonwhite) rankings (Cameron and Wycoff, 1999). Akintunde (1999) maintains that "what is amazing is the fact that these ridiculous notions are treated as inherent epistemological truths" and that "our social institutions as well as scholars in the field of education use these classifications as bases for research, equity, and educational reform to this day" (p. 3). Such knowledge reflects the values and interests of its creators.

"Consider who the major influential philosophers, writers, politicians, corporate leaders, social scientists and educational leaders (e.g., Kant, Flaubert, Churchill, Henry Ford, Weber, Dewey) have been over the course of western modernism. They have virtually all been White men. And it is they who have constructed the world we live in—named it, discussed it, and explained it," note Scheurich and Young (1997, p. 5). They further draw attention to the tendency of social institutions to qualify epistemological truths through the social construction of race; quoting Stanfield (1985, p. 389):

> [That] the White race . . . has [been] called a "privileged subset of the population" has unquestionably dominated western civilization during all of the modernist period (hundreds of years). When any group—within a large, complex civilization—significantly dominates other groups for hundreds of years, the ways of the dominant group (its epistemologies, its ontologies, its axiologies [that is, the ways of knowing what exists and what is valued]) not only become the dominant ways of that civilization, but also . . . become so embedded that they are seen as "natural" or appropriate norms rather than as historically evolved constructions.

Thus people do not question the socially constructed notions of race because they accept as "natural" that some races of people are superior and some are inferior. This is a civilizational norm; people consciously or unconsciously make decisions based on how they are conditioned through embedded, socially engineered epistemologies. A Eurocentric curriculum, for example, may not be challenged because it is considered "natural, true, and the way things are supposed to be." Until the foundations, purposes, and sociohistorical functions of this knowledge paradigm are critically examined, a continuation of the status quo at the expense of people of color is assured.

Toward Practicality: Curriculum and Instruction

If Eurocentrism is a civilizational norm, how does this norm affect community colleges? Through the current and historical inequities that affect education. When we look at school outcome data, the history of racism, classism, and exclusion in the United States stares us in the face. Unfortunately, most people in our society understand racism solely as an individual act:

> For most whites . . . racism is like murder: the concept exists but someone has to commit it in order for it to happen. This limited view of such a multilayered syndrome cultivates the sinister nature of racism and, in fact, perpetuates racist phenomena rather than eradicates them. Further, this view of racism disguises its true essence, thus allowing its tenets to proliferate. . . . Racism is a systemic, societal, institutional, omnipresent, and epistemologically embedded phenomenon that pervades every vestige of our reality [Akintunde, 1999, p. 2].

Systems of privilege and preference often create enclaves of exclusivity in schools, and these systems in turn influence our policies as well as certain demographic groups who are well served while others languish in failure or mediocrity. By way of example, the following is a testimonial by a gay white male community college instructor who faced resistance in trying to create a multicultural course at his institution. His personal account shows how policies related to epistemological Eurocentric dominance caused difficulty when he tried to diversify the English literature coursework at his community college in 2005:

> I had assumed, naively, that although a multicultural literature course did not exist at the community college where I teach, such a course would be welcomed—embraced, even. After all, educators and administrators understand by now the ravages of history and the ills of misrepresentation. They would want to correct this, right? . . . "Community colleges are well described as the most democratic enterprise in higher education, because they offer educational opportunity to anyone who wants to succeed, regardless of race, gender, age, economic circumstances, or previous learning experiences" [Modern Language Association Committee on Community Colleges, 2003, p. 165]. Such an institution would have or at least would want to have a multicultural literature course, a course that thoroughly engages the formal and contextual literary conceptualizations of power dynamics in society. A course in which all student participants are challenged to rethink and/or critique both the political structures under which they live and their own personal engagements with power. . . .

After consulting with his supervisor and obtaining her support, the instructor drafted and presented his proposed multicultural literature course to the curriculum council, which proclaimed the proposal too radical and hence rejected it:

> In order to get something passed and this course offered, I wrote up another version of the course description, which stated that the course was "an introduction to literary and cultural traditions of U.S. ethnic groups underrepresented in other literature courses. With emphases along racial and ethnic lines, students will read works by African Americans, Arab Americans, Asian Americans, Hispanic Americans . . . , Jewish Americans, and Native Americans."
>
> This description is not necessarily bad, but it is not as broad or innovative as it could be. Because the college at which I work is markedly conservative, the emphasis in this course must serve certain political purposes; in short, nothing radical can take place. . . . The college understands diversity simply as racial and ethnic inclusion, a sort of tepid affirmative action: as long as different people show up (they need not speak), diversity magically happens. . . .

As the instructor continued to explain to the curriculum council why this course was important to have on his campus, opposition mounted:

> "If literature is about representation, just speak to those who need representation" was their cry. It seemed not to be obvious to them that we do, in fact, have students from all the groups—and more—listed and that racial and ethnic representations are *not* the only subject of discussion in a multicultural literature course. My working premise is that cultures are not simply racial and/or ethnic. . . . It was obvious that my voice would not suffice. When all seemed lost, another colleague, someone tenured, spoke, and her words led to further questioning about representation, pedagogy, and multiculturalism. This colleague said that we must have all the groups on the list so that we might attract students who want to see themselves represented. She then gave a brief personal statement that silenced the entire room. "I would look for myself on that list and, if I couldn't find myself, I wouldn't take the course." My colleague spoke as a woman of color, something that I was, ostensibly, unable to do. She brilliantly used the language in the room to help the course proposal pass: she used the language of "diversity," or liberal pluralism, to facilitate the understanding that a course such as this one must exist. Her presence and voice took away the negative energy circulating in the room, and the proposal passed. . . . It seemed that some of my colleagues in the room now understood: [that] multiple voices are necessary for contextualization, interrogation, and healing and that restricting a multicultural course to the supposed identity of one or another student population cannot produce learning [Clem, 2005, pp. 125–129].

This testimonial makes clear that systems of privilege and preference often create enclaves of exclusivity in schools, and these systems influence our policies through solutions based on limited visions related to a Euro-centric viewpoint. Multicultural curriculum changes in the instructor's story would not be considered "radical" if a diversity-affirmative ethical orientation existed in schooling contexts. This instructor realized that his colleagues did not have a similar viewpoint as his and they did not understand the complexities of "the ravages of history and the ills of misrepresentation" in society. They did not understand the need for a clear examination, through deep introspection, of the disfranchisement and "deculturalized" legacies that many ethnic, gender, class, caste, age, ability, sexuality, and other groups continue to experience in this country (Spring, 2006). If his colleagues understood why a multicultural curriculum is vital to hearing the voices of the diverse students in his school and how diversity-affirming ethics benefit us all, then they would have approved his original course proposal without reservation. If diversity-affirming ethics guided institutional decision making and tenets of critical epistemology were readily embraced, the choice would have been easy. However, the systems of privilege and preference at this school caused people to dismiss the importance of such a course and exclude whole groups, watering down the curriculum to include a limited range of voices. Questioning the value of the proposed course revealed that the voices of the majority of this institution were operating based on "whiteness" as culturally, systemically, and epistemologically privileged.

Howard (2006), a multicultural theorist and antiracist activist, explains that the roots of racism and social dominance may be examined through a paradigm that consists of three components: the assumption of rightness, the luxury of ignorance, and the legacy of privilege. The curriculum council and members of this community college operated on the assumption of rightness when they explained that this course was "too radical" and that there was no need for a course that addressed so many groups of people. Furthermore, the members of this community college did not share a "knowledge base" to substantiate the need for such a course and displayed a limited perspective, which is part of the "luxury of ignorance." Persons who are members of the dominant group do not necessarily need to educate themselves beyond the group's paradigm. At the college in question, there was a general impulse to keep the proposed course from being accepted, and this resistance relates to the "legacy of privilege." Such privilege may be observed in this instance because, as a collective group who also held the majority perspective, the instructors at this institution could substantiate their determination of what is valued or not valued, and this resistance relates to the privileged axiology in operation (Scheurich and Young, 1997). Therefore, this is a fine example of white racism in practice: no individual is committing a racist act, but institutional epistemological racism is in operation nonetheless.

Another important question related to the instructor's story is what the outcome might have been if there had not been a person of color to question the reasoning of the faculty council. We doubt that the course would have been adopted, especially as a course examining the variety of voices that was intended. The voices of people of color are necessary in order to assist in the eradication of institutional epistemological racism. The fact that the African American faculty member's voice was acknowledged and acted on may mean a couple of things. First, in public institutions, white people often get squeamish about discussions of race, gender, and homosexuality and therefore often brush over such discussions when a person to whom the subject is salient enters the argument. So the council members may have been stopped in their tracks when the faculty member of color stated her opinion. Second, adoption may be due not to any deeper understanding of the issue but rather to the faculty council's not wanting to be perceived as "racist, sexist, homophobic, classist," or the like.

Many important meanings come out of this story. The community college faculty member who drafted the multicultural course and one who spoke on behalf of the course may be viewed as allies in laying the groundwork for acceptance of the multicultural literature course, albeit unintentionally. Allies are nonetheless helpful in the development of multicultural education through the eradication of institutional epistemological racism. If these decisions were to be guided by a diversity ethic, considerations of rightness and wrongness would be based on the principle that diversity is positive, advantageous, and helpful to individuals, institutions, and society as a whole. And to effectively eradicate epistemological racism, allies must unite to make changes within the institution.

Diversifying curricula and instruction can promote a positive value of diversity and can open up a dialogue about the historical legacy and potential negative impact of a Eurocentric epistemology and how that contributes to the perpetuation of social and economic orders. Conversations about the benefits of diversity for all members of society can begin. Guided by a diversity-affirming ethical and critical epistemological understanding, educational leaders in community colleges can be vanguards for supporting the diversification curriculum and instructional practices.

Institutional Access and Opportunity

One major mission and practice of the community college is open access, which plays an important democratizing role in the American postsecondary system (Dowd, 2003). Historically, community colleges have extended education to the vast majority of American youths and adults. The Truman Commission Report provides an early vision that currently permeates the system of community colleges:

> If the ladder of educational opportunity rises high at the doors of some youth and scarcely rises at all at the doors of others, while at the same time formal

education is made a prerequisite to occupational and social advance, then education may become the means, not of eliminating race and class distinctions, but of deepening and solidifying them. *It is obvious, then, that free and universal access to education, in terms of interest, ability, and need of the student, must be a major goal of American education* [U.S. President's Commission on Higher Education, 1947, p. 36; emphasis in the original].

American education must provide opportunities for all students to better themselves, and community colleges are an important entryway into higher education for the advancement of all students and particularly students of color. If community colleges are guided by a diversity ethic, considerations of access and opportunities support the principle that diversity is positive, advantageous, and helpful to individuals, institutions, and society. For the past two decades, low-income students, women, African Americans, Latinos, immigrants, and working adults have made up the majority of students attending community colleges (Bragg, 2001). However, educational institutions struggle with providing successful educational equity outcomes for diverse students. For instance, "more than 45 percent of the Hispanics in Arizona have less than a high school education, and only 5.7 percent have a bachelor's degree. For myriad reasons, many Hispanics drop out of school before they reach the ninth grade. American Indians do not fare much better. The levels of educational attainment of African-Americans are better than Hispanics, but fall far short of the educational levels of Whites" (Flores and Hagan, 2008, p. 16).

Since the community college population is very diverse, community colleges have the opportunity to go beyond the standard Eurocentric epistemological practices to foster the implementation of diversity ethics in the advancement of equity.

Equity is an important goal on the community college agenda for democratizing American higher education. Dowd (2003, p. 93) sums up how equity plays an important role in community colleges yet struggles to advance a true diversity ethic of equity due to public funding and political and economic challenges: "With open admissions policies and diverse student bodies, community colleges 'in an idealized sense, represent higher education's commitment to democracy' (Rhoads and Valadez, 1996, p. 7). . . . [However], in the 1990s, the ideal of the community college as an agent of democracy was undermined by cuts in public funding and privatization of the public sector."

Community colleges' historical commitment to equity must also work toward "[reducing] socioeconomic and racial disparities in student enrollment, graduation rates, and participation in programs leading to high wage employment" (Harbour and Jaquette, 2007, p. 197). However, for diversity ethics and equity outcomes to become fully realized in community colleges, it is important to promote an equity agenda that fosters an epistemologically sound practice to foster diversity.

Toward Closure

Our brief exploration of curriculum and instruction and institutional access does not cover all areas where diversity-affirming ethics and a critical epistemology might affect institutional decision making in community colleges. For example, school climate concerns, faculty diversification, and the politics of knowledge production are not thoroughly discussed. However, what does clearly emerge is a need to consider whether decision making promotes status quo perpetuation or positive social change. What matters is the curriculum and how it is taught, as well as who gets access and opportunity to reap the benefits of higher education. Also important are our value systems and our awareness of the limits of our knowledge paradigms. Do we value what is different, or do we want to assimilate it? Do we understand the limited nature of our knowledge paradigms and how they are historically and contextually constructed? Do we actively seek out and integrate the diversity that just might be vital for institutional and societal sustainability?

Community colleges present a prime opportunity to mitigate the tensions between the desire for education as social justice and the realities of access for historically marginalized populations. If institutional decision making in community colleges is guided by diversity-affirming ethics and a critical epistemological orientation, perhaps we may take giant leaps toward reconciling oppressive conditions that originate in legacies of power and privilege. Creating a "hard" infrastructure—diversity in curriculum and instruction, political representation, a leveling of economic power, allocation of resources to make the conditions of the least well-off the best they can be (Rawls, 1971), and an educational policy context that grants significant agency to local actors and institutions in the process of empowered curriculum making—is critical to a larger multicultural peace and social justice agenda.

Guiding Questions

1. Why do diversity-affirming ethics and a critical epistemological orientation promote social justice at community colleges? Examine how they can be or have been integrated in your institutional setting.
2. Analyze the story by the community college professor in this chapter, and explain the different facets of a critical epistemological perspective at work.
3. Why is it important to understand our knowledge paradigms and how they are historically and contextually constructed?
4. How should we actively seek out and integrate the ethnic, socioeconomic, gender, sexual orientation, and physical ability diversities that exist on our community college campuses for future societal democratic sustainability?

References

Akintunde, O. "White Racism, White Privilege, and the Social Construction of Race: Moving from a Modernist to Postmodernist Multicultural Education." *Multicultural Perspectives*, 1999, *1*(4), 2–8.

Akintunde, O. "Diversity.com: Teaching an Online Course on White Racism and Multiculturalism." *Multicultural Perspectives*, 2006, *8*(2), 35–45.

Banks, J. A. "Approaches to Multicultural Curriculum Reform." In J. A. Banks and C. A. McGee Banks (eds.), *Multicultural Education: Issues and Perspectives* (4th ed.). New York: Wiley, 2001.

Blackburn, S. (ed.). *The Oxford Dictionary of Philosophy*. Oxford: Oxford University Press, 1994.

Bragg, D. "Community College Access, Mission, and Outcomes: Considering Intriguing Intersections and Challenges." *Peabody Journal of Education*, 2001, *76*, 93–116.

Cameron, S. C., and Wycoff, S. M. "The Destructive Nature of the Term *Race*: Growing Beyond a False Paradigm." *Journal of Counseling and Development*, 1999, *77*, 277–284.

Carspecken, P. F. *Critical Ethnography in Educational Research: A Theoretical and Practical Guide*. London: Routledge, 1996.

Clem, B. "Pedagogy of a Radical Multiculturalism." *MELUS*, 2005, *30*, 123–138.

Davis, G. W. "Why Presidents and Trustees Should Care About Ethics." In D. M. Hellmich (ed.), *Ethical Leadership in the Community College: Bridging Theory and Daily Practice*. Bolton, Mass.: Anker, 2007.

Delpit, L. "The Silenced Dialogue: Power and Pedagogy in Educating Other People's Children." *Harvard Educational Review*, 1988, *58*, 280–298.

Dowd, A. "From Access to Outcome Equity: Revitalizing the Democratic Mission of the Community College." *Annals of the American Academy of Political and Social Science*, 2003, *586*(1), 92–119.

Flores, R., and Hagan, B. "It's About Access." *Diverse Issues in Higher Education*, 2008, *25*(10), 16.

Harbour, C. P., and Jaquette, O. "Advancing an Equity Agenda at the Community College in an Age of Privatization, Performance Accountability, and Marketization." *Equity and Excellence in Education*, 2007, *40*, 197–207.

Howard, G. *We Can't Teach What We Don't Know: White Teachers, Multiracial School* (2nd ed.). New York: Teachers College Press, 2006.

Ladson-Billings, G., and Tate, W. F., IV. "Toward a Critical Race Theory of Education." *Teachers College Record*, 1995, *97*(1), 47–68.

Modern Language Association Committee on Community Colleges. "Considering Community Colleges: Advice to Graduate Students and Job Seekers." *Profession*, 2003, 164–171.

Rawls, J. *A Theory of Justice*. Cambridge, Mass.: Harvard University Press, 1971.

Rhoads, R. A., and Valadez, J. R. *Democracy, Multiculturalism, and the Community College: A Critical Perspective*. New York: Routledge, 1996.

Scheurich, J., and Young, M. "Coloring Epistemologies: Are Our Research Epistemologies Racially Biased?" *Educational Researcher*, 1997, *26*(4), 4–16.

Sleeter, C. E., and Grant, C. A. *Making Choices for Multicultural Education: Five Approaches to Race, Class, and Gender* (3rd ed.). New York: Wiley, 1999.

Spring, J. *Deculturalization and the Struggle for Equality: A Brief History of the Education of Dominated Cultures in the United States* (5th ed.). New York: McGraw-Hill, 2006.

Stanfield, J. H., The ethnocentric basis of social science knowledge production. *Review of Research in Education*, 1985, *12*, 387–415.

U.S. President's Commission on Higher Education. *Higher Education for Democracy*, Vol. I, *Establishing the Goals*, Washington, D.C.: Government Printing Office, 1947.

Wallin, D. "Ethical Leadership: The Role of the President." In D. M. Hellmich (ed.), *Ethical Leadership in the Community College: Bridging Theory and Daily Practice.* Bolton, Mass.: Anker, 2007.

ANTONETTE ARAGON is assistant professor in the School of Education at Colorado State University. Her research focuses on multicultural teacher education, antiracist multicultural education, and the examination of marginalized students.

EDWARD J. BRANTMEIER is assistant professor in the School of Education at Colorado State University. His research focus includes multicultural peace education, cultural conflict, and cultural change.

5

This chapter presents an overview of student affairs in community colleges, developmental theories related to ethical and moral development, a review of the major ethical codes and standards for student affairs professionals, and a framework for resolving ethical dilemmas. It also includes some brief practitioner scenarios for analysis.

Ethical Issues for Community College Student Affairs Professionals

Anne M. Hornak

Community colleges have historically been a major gateway to higher education for many students. Students enroll in community college programs and courses for multiple reasons: closeness to home, financial issues, job retraining, remedial work, plans to transfer to a four-year institution, and a love of learning. These divergent goals make community college student populations among the most diverse in higher education (Cohen and Brawer, 2008; Hellmich, 2007). With this diversity come challenges to the institution and the student affairs leaders. This chapter explores the developmental theories related to ethical development of students and provides an overview of student affairs at community colleges and the ethical responsibilities of those professionals. This overview will include looking at the codes of three professional organizations and a framework for resolving ethical dilemmas.

Community College Students

It is important to begin with an explanation of who our community college students are. Whom do the student affairs practitioners, faculty, and other leaders work with on a daily basis? Community college students are unique in that their educational goals can vary greatly. In the same course, a faculty member may have middle-aged single parents, recent high school graduates, laid-off factory workers, older lifelong learners, and retired community members. On the surface, the diverse student body may not seem an issue,

NEW DIRECTIONS FOR COMMUNITY COLLEGES, no. 148, Winter 2009 © 2009 Wiley Periodicals, Inc.
Published online in Wiley InterScience (www.interscience.wiley.com) • DOI: 10.1002/cc.386

but institutionally, it can be difficult to make decisions on a daily basis about curricular changes, programming needs, and resource allocation with such divergent educational goals (Helfgot, 2005).

We have historically thought of community colleges as heavily populated by nontraditional students (ages twenty-four and up), but in a 2008 report by the American Association of Community Colleges (AACC), the authors found that more than 45 percent of the student populations were traditionally aged students, eighteen to twenty-three. This finding presents an interesting and exciting opportunity for community college student affairs professionals as they think about how to meet the needs of this student population. Furthermore, most community college students are balancing more than just school, which means that their time on campus is almost exclusively limited to classroom instruction. Since most student affairs professionals are not traditional classroom instructors, their access to and interactions with students may be limited to times of the year when needs are highest—for example, during registration, financial aid renewals, or situations of crisis (Community College Survey, 2008). This presents an interesting ethical dilemma of how to reach community college students who need assistance but are on campus for limited amounts of time. The purpose of this chapter is not to explore how to engage with community college students outside the classroom, but as I address the ethical responsibilities and standards of the student services units, it is an important fact to remember.

Developmental Models for Ethical and Moral Reasoning

The theoretical literature on ethical and moral reasoning on which student affairs practitioners rely has largely been grounded in the fields of student development and educational psychology. Looking at ethics through a student development lens, however, being an ethical practitioner involves addressing ever-changing complex issues and problems. Presenting the developmental issues of ethical and moral development is important because training for student affairs professionals is not consistent across a given discipline. Moreover, many professionals who work in student affairs have not completed a master's degree program, where much of this knowledge is usually acquired. Optimal student affairs education should also involve leadership development, and a part of being a good leader is being an ethical leader and mentor (Starratt, 2004). Ethics is unique in that the development of an ethical mind-set usually comes with experiences and making decisions under stressful circumstances, which can later be revisited and analyzed. Community colleges are engrossed in an ever-changing environment that tests the ethical development of leaders and practitioners on a daily basis. Many theorists have contributed to our body of knowledge regarding ethical development. The classic work by William Perry (1970) provides insight into how students view both sources of knowledge and positions of right and wrong. Perry's theory posits a series of cognitive and ethical positions that is based on a dualistic view of the world (right versus wrong, black versus white) and develops a more contextual understanding of knowledge that recognizes that multiple data sources need to be considered. The theory helps us understand that ethical decision making is complex and that if the individuals making the decisions are not complex thinkers, decisions could be dualistic and not in the best interest of the population.

Karen Kitchener and Patricia King (1994) provide a seven-stage model of reflective judgment that is based on the work of John Dewey (1933), who stated that a goal of education is being a reflective thinker. They define reflective thinking as the ability to use reasoning and evidence in solving problems. The model provides a developmental framework for how individuals resolve ill-structured problems based on their epistemological and cognitive developmental capacities. For practitioners, this framework can be important when thinking about ethical decisions because many of these decisions are made with incomplete and even conflicting data (Kitchener and King, 1994).

Lawrence Kohlberg (1984) and Carol Gilligan (1993) have also provided seminal theories that have advanced how we look at moral and ethical decision making in a developmental way. Kohlberg's theory of moral development was initially based on a study of adolescent boys and guided by the methodology of Jean Piaget's ([1932] 1977) work with the moral development of children. The theory is a six-stage model based on the notion that moral development, which is the basis for ethical behavior, is a lifelong process. The theory postulates that moral development is largely based on the notion that justice is the essential factor of moral reasoning (Kohlberg, 1984). Gilligan also provided a theory on moral development, but her initial study was based on women participants, and she criticized Kohlberg for leaving women out of the inquiry. Gilligan's research proposed a stage theory of moral development for women based on the ethic of care rather than on an ethic of justice. Gilligan argued that women are different in their moral reasoning and not well represented in Kohlberg's stage theory. Gilligan's theory has three major divisions, similar to Kohlberg's. The biggest difference, however, is that Gilligan posited that transitions are fueled by changes in self as opposed to cognitive capability. Her work advances the notion that men and women make decisions differently.

Other important theorists have contributed to our knowledge about moral and ethical decision making. James Fowler (1980) proposed a theory about spiritual development that is related to the Kohlberg and Gilligan theories. Robert Kegan (1982), George Herbert Mead (1934), Abraham Maslow (1954), Jürgen Habermas (1979), Nel Noddings (1984), James Mark Baldwin (1913), and many other theorists and philosophers have expanded our understanding of how individuals develop the capacity to make ethical decisions, given the complexity of the problem and within the context of education. Shapiro and Stefkovich (2005) offer another perspective on complex dilemmas. Their theory presents four paradigms for considering challenging ethical decisions: the ethics of justice, critique, care, and the profession. The theories already explored in this chapter are inclusive of the ethics of justice, critique, and care, but often we do not look at the ethics of the profession. Understanding the formal codes of the profession and the standards of the field that guide our work as educators is a critical part of ethical decision making. Shapiro and Stefkovich argue that there is not one best ethical paradigm but instead, "by using different models [and paradigms], professionals will be able to work through their own personal and professional ethical codes" (p. 9). In addition, they argue that understanding our own personal codes of ethics and standards of practice will help us be the most effective professionals we can be. I would also assert that an understanding of our own institutional mission and values is also important in making ethical decisions.

The Student Affairs Profession

The student affairs and student development profession is best understood as the collaboration of a number of diverse fields, and the goal of the professionals who hold these positions is the personal development of students (Barr, Desler, and Associates, 2000). Student development professionals work in a variety of college units: academic advising, admissions, financial aid, enrollment management, registration, and student activities, to name a few (Komives, Woodard, and Associates, 2003). At community colleges, student services professionals work in traditional student affairs units but do so with a much different student population and mission (Dougherty, 2003). The student population at community colleges, as described earlier, is not only diverse but also changes as the social conditions of the community and the larger environment change. This creates unique challenges for student affairs professionals as they develop programs and services to meet the needs of these students. This also creates unique challenges to addressing ethical issues that arise on a daily basis (Anderson, Harbour, and Davies, 2007).

Ethical Responsibilities for Student Affairs Professionals

The ethical responsibilities for student affairs professionals at community colleges could be simplistically described as the holistic development of students, helping them grow academically, socially, physically, mentally, and spiritually. Yet as the daily work of student affairs professionals is carried out, their responsibilities are much more complex than just the holistic development of students. The diversity of the student population and the diversity of the work create an unpredictable environment when making decisions about student learning and institutional priorities. Community college leaders often face situations in which the problem is ill-defined but the implications stretch beyond one office and may affect multiple campus entities and the larger community (Anderson, Harbour, and Davies, 2007).

Practitioner Scenarios

Thinking about ethics from a practical standpoint is important in comprehending the complexities of most situations. Here are two vignettes to illustrate the complexities involved with most ethical issues. Assume that you are the director of admissions at a large open-access community college. A large number of the admitted students are ill-prepared for college-level work and require many resources in tutoring and writing assistance. The college has minimal resources for tutoring and academic assistance for students. You feel that the college has a responsibility to provide academic assistance to all admitted students; a student's admission is comparable to a contract stating that the student can be successful at this school. The admission rate at the college is very good, but the fall-to-fall retention rate is below 30 percent. The dean of students sends you an e-mail stating the new admission goals of the college, and they are far above the current level the college can accommodate. The e-mail outlines a plan if the admission requirements are not met that includes cutting staff in your office. This new plan presents a conflict among your personal values, your perception of the mission of an open-access institution, and resource allocation at the college. How do you proceed, given this conflict?

In the second scenario, assume that you are the director of diversity programs at a community college in a large urban area. You are responsible for collegewide diversity programming. You also work closely with the community outreach office in providing diversity training for local businesses. The manager of one of the businesses that uses this community program approaches you after the last task force meeting. She wants you to conduct a more extensive training program for her business and has offered to pay you. You make a nice salary at the college but are interested in doing more in the community on a consulting basis. Your college has a conflict-of-interest policy for faculty, but it is a loose policy and not clearly spelled out for administrators. Is this a conflict of interest that should not be pursued? How do you handle this situation?

Professional Codes and Standards

Many professions are regulated by national or state licensure or certifications that provide guidance on the ethical codes and professional standards that guide work in those professions. The codes and standards are minimum guidelines that provide a paradigm of ethical responsibility (Shapiro and Stefkovich, 2005) that is unique to each profession. Individuals have their own moral and ethical codes that guide their lives, and many times these codes are more virtuous and aspirational than the minimum standards set by the professions. It is the combination of professional codes and personal codes of ethics that guide our daily lives and work.

Shapiro and Stefkovich (2005) discuss the ethics of the profession as the weaving together of the ethics of justice, care, and critique, "much like a tapestry" (p. 19). The ethics of the profession, as framed by these authors, puts ethical guidelines into the context of educational settings. The issues faced by educators can differ from other professions. The codes specifically highlight these unique challenges, such as managing dual relationships between faculty and students, working within one's own competencies, and maintaining confidentiality of student records. There are many organizations that represent the work of student development practitioners, and my focus is on the American Association for Community Colleges, American College Personnel Association (ACPA), and National Association of Student Personnel Administrators (NASPA). These three organizations and their affiliate councils, standing committees, commission directorates, and knowledge communities represent the work of community college student development professionals internationally. Furthermore, all three organizations have promulgated ethical standards that have become the leading models for professionals.

The three codes of ethics, standards of professional practice, or core values have many similarities to guide the image and character of professionals working with college students. It is important to remember the unique nature of the work and the diversity of the students who interact with community college student development professionals. The work is complex and can differ on a daily basis. The guideposts provided by the professional organizations address issues of image and character and embody the "highest moral ideals of the profession" (Shapiro and Stefkovich, 2005, p. 34). The codes are limited in their responsiveness to the daily decisions that practitioners face, but they still offer guidance regarding values and standards.

Each professional code was designed to provide guidance to student affairs professionals in their daily work with students. They also differ in the language and detail provided regarding behavior. The ACPA code highlights five foundations: "act to benefit others, promote justice, respect autonomy, be faithful, and do no harm" (ACPA, 2006, para. 4). In addition, ACPA provides four ethical standards that give clearer guidance about behavior: "professional responsibility and competence, responsibility to the institution, student learning and development, and responsibility to society" (para. 6). The NASPA *Standards of Professional Practice* (1990) provide more specific guidance regarding ethical standards and behaviors. The statement highlights eighteen standards for professional conduct: professional services, agreement with institutional mission and goals, management of institutional resources, employment relationship, conflicts of interest, legal authority, equal consideration and treatment of others, student behavior, integrity of information and research, confidentiality, research involving human subjects, representation of professional competence, selection and promotion practices, references, job definitions and performance evaluation, campus community, professional development, and assessment.

Finally, the AACC core values highlight seven areas that guide the decision making of AACC leaders and staff: "integrity, excellence, leadership, learning, diversity, commitment, and connectedness" (2006, para. 6). Clearly, the three codes provide varying degrees of specificity and scope regarding professional behavior. The goal of the codes is to provide abstract guidelines for ethical decision making. The standards are not meant to be prescriptive but rather to provide direction for making complex ethical decisions by practitioners. For example, one of the standards in all three codes addresses individual responsibility to follow institutional policies and procedures. Institutional rules and regulations are an important mechanism for accountability. It becomes increasingly complex when these policies create a conflict with student learning and success. College employees can use their ethical codes and professional organizations as sources for consultation.

Ethical Decision Making

Theoretical frameworks and paradigms provide evidence that individuals make complex decisions differently based on their developmental level. As practitioners, we cannot be assured that all ethical dilemmas will have solutions. The codes we use to guide behavior often do not recognize the true complexities of these decisions. However, the systematic use of an ethical decision-making model provides steps for analyzing paradoxical dilemmas. There are many models and guides that could be employed when making an ethical decision, and most are grounded in psychological and counseling models. Corey Schneider, Corey, and Callanan (2003) provide a ten-step model for making ethical decisions. This model was selected for inclusion in this discussion because of its holistic approach and its endorsement of consultation with other professionals and ethical and legal codes. The model, while grounded in the counseling literature, provides a comprehensive framework for making an ethical decision across many disciplines. As you read the steps highlighted by these theorists, it becomes apparent that ethical decisions should not be made in a vacuum and that the inclusion of diverse perspectives and multiple forms of evidence, such as consulting with other professionals and ethical codes, is crucial.

The first step under this model is to recognize the problem or dilemma. This involves gathering as much information as possible about the situation. Practitioners need to clarify whether the conflict is ethical, legal, professional, moral, or a combination. Most problems are complex and involve more than one individual, office, or entity, and it is important that recognition of the problem involves gathering objective facts about the situation and all the individuals involved. The second step is to identify the potential issues involved. This entails listing and describing the critical issues and evaluating the rights and responsibilities of the parties affected by the situation. The third step is to review the relevant ethical codes that inform your professional needs. Consulting ethical codes and standards may offer a possible solution to the problem. Moreover, most professional organizations have hotlines or ethics officers that can serve as resources in making an ethical decision. The fourth step is to know the applicable laws and regulations. Many ethical dilemmas have legal implications, and a holistic approach must acknowledge this dimension. Knowing the relevant state and federal laws can help in resolving the issue. Furthermore, having a clear understanding of the rules and regulations of your institution is important, and consulting your institutional attorney can be beneficial. The fifth step is to obtain consultation, which may be the most important step in the process. Ethical decisions should not be made in a vacuum, and as professionals, we need to obtain diverse perspectives on the problems we face on our campuses. The sixth step is to consider possible and probable courses of action. Listing a variety of courses of action to identify the best course can give some perspective on the complexity of the dilemma. The seventh step is to enumerate the consequences of various decisions. Each decision has a consequence, and asking how this may affect students, parents, community, faculty, and other stakeholders may lead to a better decision. The eighth step in the model is to select what appears to be the best course of action: it is important to consider all information carefully, but ultimately a decision must be made. The final two steps are implementation and evaluation. It is always easier when reflecting on a decision to see what you did right and what could have been done better, and by continuing to review the decision and evaluate the consequences, professionals become better decision makers and more ethical practitioners.

Conclusion

This chapter presented a snapshot of community college students, the developmental perspectives in which individuals make moral and ethical decisions, the work that community college student affairs professionals do, and a ten-step model to making ethical decisions. The unique nature of educational institutions and the stakeholders affected by these complex decisions makes it difficult to prescribe how these decisions should be made. Rather it is important to remember that the best interests of the students should be the foremost goal. It is also important to remember to be true to yourself and to the mission of the institution. Finally, there are many tools that should be used during the decision-making process. It is the ethical obligation of practitioners to understand and employ those tools and resources. To help develop professional practice, I encourage readers to apply the ten-step decision-making model to the two practitioner scenarios presented in this chapter. By carefully examining the facts given in each scenario and then addressing them using the model, student affairs professionals may continue to develop their decision-making skills in an area that offers up some of the thorniest dilemmas.

Guiding Questions

- How do our decisions affect our colleagues and students?
- Ethical dilemmas are complex; in what ways does working as a student affairs professional in a community college add to the complexity?
- What role does understanding moral and ethical development play in ethical decision making?
- What kinds of professional development opportunities can be created to help individuals make good ethical decisions?

References

American Association of Community Colleges. *AACC Mission: Building a Nation of Learners by Advancing America's Community Colleges*. Washington D.C.: American Association of Community Colleges, 2006.

American Association of Community Colleges. *Fast Facts*. [http://www.aacc.nche.edu/AboutCC/Pages/fastfacts.aspx]. Oct. 23, 2008.

American College Personnel Association (ACPA). *Ethics Statement and Resources*. Washington, D.C.: American College Personnel Association, 2006.

Anderson, S. K., Harbour, C. P., and Davies, T. G. "Professional Ethical Identity Development and Community College Leadership." In D. M. Hellmich (ed.), *Ethical Leadership in the Community College: Bridging Theory and Daily Practice*. Bolton, Mass.: Anker, 2007.

Baldwin, J. M. *Social and Ethical Interpretations in Mental Development* (5th ed.). New York: Macmillan, 1913.

Barr, M. J., Desler, M. K., and Associates. *The Handbook of Student Affairs Administration*. San Francisco: Jossey-Bass, 2000.

Cohen, A. M., and Brawer, F. B. *The American Community College* (5th ed.). San Francisco: Jossey-Bass, 2008.

Community College Survey of Student Engagement. *High Expectations, High Support*. Austin: University of Texas at Austin Community College Leadership Program, 2008.

Corey Schneider, M., Corey, G., and Callanan, P. *Instructor's Resources Manual for Issues and Ethics in the Helping Professions*. Boston: Brooks/Cole, 2003.

Dewey, J. *How We Think: A Restatement of the Relation of Reflective Thinking to the Educative Process*. Lexington, Mass.: Heath, 1933.

Dougherty, K. "The Community College: The Origins, Impacts, and Futures of a Contradictory Institution." In J. Ballantine and J. Spade (eds.), *Schools and Society*. Belmont, Calif.: Wadsworth, 2003.

Fowler, J. "Moral Stages and the Development of Faith." In L. Kohlberg and B. Munsey (eds.), *Moral Development, Moral Education*. Birmingham, Ala.: Religious Education Press, 1980.

Gilligan, C. *In a Different Voice: Psychological Theory and Women's Development*. Cambridge, Mass.: Harvard University Press, 1993.

Habermas, J. *Communication and the Evolution of Society* (T. McCarthy, trans.). Boston: Beacon Press, 1979.

Helfgot, S. R. "Core Values and Major Issues in Student Affairs Practice: What Really Matters?" In S. R. Helfgot and M. M. Culp (eds.). *What Matters in Community College Student Affairs.* New Directions for Community Colleges, no. 131. San Francisco: Jossey-Bass, 2005.

Hellmich, D. M. (ed.). *Ethical Leadership in the Community College: Bridging Theory and Daily Practice.* Bolton, Mass.: Anker, 2007.

Kegan, R. *The Evolving Self: Problem and Process in Human Development.* Cambridge, Mass.: Harvard University Press, 1982.

Kitchener, K. S., and King, P. M. *Developing Reflective Judgment: Understanding and Promoting Intellectual Growth and Critical Thinking in Adolescents and Adults.* San Francisco: Jossey-Bass, 1994.

Kohlberg, L. *The Psychology of Moral Development.* San Francisco: HarperOne, 1984.

Komives, S. R., Woodard, D. B., Jr., and Associates. *Student Services: A Handbook for the Profession* (4th ed.). San Francisco: Jossey-Bass, 2003.

Maslow, A. *Motivation and Personality.* New York: HarperCollins, 1954.

Mead, G. H. *Mind, Self, and Society.* Chicago: University of Chicago Press, 1934.

NASPA. *Standards of Professional Practice.* Washington, D.C.: NASPA, 1990.

Noddings, N. *Caring: A Feminine Approach to Ethics and Moral Education.* Berkeley: University of California Press, 1984.

Perry, W. G. *Intellectual and Ethical Development in the College Years.* New York: Holt, Rinehart and Winston, 1970.

Piaget, J. *The Moral Judgment of the Child* (M. Gabain, trans.). Harmondsworth, UK: Penguin, 1977. (Originally published 1932.)

Shapiro, J. P., and Stefkovich, J. A. *Ethical Leadership and Decision Making in Education.* Mahwah, N.J.: Erlbaum, 2005.

Starratt, R. J. *Ethical Leadership.* San Francisco: Jossey-Bass, 2004.

ANNE M. HORNAK is assistant professor of educational leadership at Central Michigan University.

The blending of technology and education introduces ethical issues for colleges. In particular, those involved with online education may encounter unique dilemmas that have collegewide implications. In order for ethical decisions to be made in regard to online education, colleges must cultivate a culture of trust, define clearly the correct and incorrect usages of electronic material, and develop a clear understanding of privacy in the college's online environment.

Ethics in an Online Environment

Regina L. Garza Mitchell

Community colleges are known for their emphasis on teaching and learning and for their ability to make rapid changes depending on market and student demands, including keeping up with technological changes. Thus it is no surprise that the majority of students taking online courses do so at two-year institutions (Allen and Seaman, 2008). This blending of technology within an educational context has resulted in numerous structural and procedural changes at community colleges. The integration of technology brings about many positive changes, but as technology becomes more ingrained into the college structure, new ethical dilemmas may arise.

Online education is closely associated with change. The rapid pace of change in regard to technology alone requires those involved in online education to act quickly when making decisions and to implement change on a regular basis. As with any aspect of leadership, bringing about change requires a strong ethical underpinning in order to make decisions that are in the best interest of the college and its culture (Hellmich, 2007). For ethical decisions to be made in regard to online education, colleges must cultivate a culture of trust, clearly define the correct and incorrect usages of electronic material, and develop a clear understanding of privacy in the college's online environment. This development requires institutional familiarity with and shared understanding of laws and common practices regarding online materials, particularly as these issues spill over into on-campus activities. This chapter explores issues of trust and the appropriate use of materials in an online environment through the use of scenarios. The scenarios presented here derive from actual events at various colleges and highlight

issues faced by community college administrators and faculty who work with online education.

Issues of Trust

Behavior in a college is guided by cultural norms that presumably promote its mission, values, and ethical behavior (Hellmich, 2007). As new practices are incorporated, they may not automatically fit into an existing norm, so colleges will have to develop trust that these practices are necessary. Trust is associated with physical presence, a crucial element that is lacking in the online environment (Myskja, 2008). Thus several factors impair the level of trust associated with online education. The following scenarios provide examples of mistrust about online education.

Scenario 1

Large Multicampus Community College (LMCC) has been involved with online education for the past ten years. It developed a robust online education program in which five complete degree programs and more than two hundred courses are offered to students every year in an online format. Both full-time and adjunct faculty members teach these courses only after successfully completing an intense eight-week professional development course that requires a commitment of ten to twenty hours per week, and the faculty are required to retake the training every two years. This faculty development in online teaching covers pedagogical concepts in addition to technology training. Full- and part-time instructors who are hired to teach on campus have a different training requirement. The on-campus faculty must complete a new faculty academy that is offered as a series of six hourlong sessions one Friday per month, and they have up to two years to complete the training. Despite the intense training requirement for online courses and consensus that online courses at LMCC are of high quality, face-to-face courses remain the standard of comparison. In addition, instructors who teach all courses online are still required to host on-site campus hours two days per week. Despite the long-term and widespread use of online education at LMCC, distrust still exists regarding the work of online faculty relative to on-campus faculty. The latter group is seen as providing the norm for teaching and learning.

Scenario 2

Rural Valley Community College (RVCC) first developed online courses a little over ten years ago. It currently offers approximately eighty courses online but no complete programs. RVCC frequently has trouble finding faculty to teach courses online. Several full-time faculty members teach online courses as overload, but the majority of online instructors are adjuncts. Full-time faculty who teach online are encouraged, but not required, to complete a training course prior to teaching online, and their online courses are not regularly evaluated by students or administrators. Adjunct faculty members who teach online are required to complete two training courses selected from a list of options, one prior to teaching and the second during their first year of teaching. Their courses are evaluated according to the same schedule as on-campus adjunct faculty members. Full- and part-time faculty who teach on campus are not required to attend any type of faculty development training, though one in-service day is held each semester. The in-service is required for full-time faculty and optional for adjunct faculty members.

These two scenarios demonstrate a distrust of online education despite its decadelong presence at both colleges. Scenario 1 presents an institution with vastly different requirements for faculty who teach online as opposed to face-to-face. Instructors who teach online at LMCC are required to be trained on both the technology and pedagogical concepts *prior* to teaching, while faculty who teach on campus may take up to two years to complete training. Scenario 1 reflects a distrust of teaching and learning in an online environment. Scenario 2 presumes that instructors who have taught full time teach well and that they are also able to do so in an online environment, whereas adjunct faculty are deemed ill-prepared for teaching online. There is also a suggestion that adjunct faculty members are in greater need of training than their full-time counterparts. Both scenarios suggest an inherent assumption that if an instructor teaches in a physical classroom, learning will occur despite the faculty member's ability to teach or the extent of the instructor's prior training in teaching strategies. This assumption is strengthened by the decision at RVCC not to evaluate online courses taught by full-time faculty members.

The 1990s saw the adoption of a learning paradigm (Barr and Tagg, 1995) and a movement toward becoming learning colleges (O'Banion, 1997). Online education favors constructivist and cognitive approaches to teaching that align with the learning college philosophy (Meyer, 2002). The bulk of the literature about online teaching and learning focuses on collaboration and developing learning communities (e.g., Palloff and Pratt, 1999, 2003, 2004, 2007, 2008), discussion (for example, Bender, 2003; Collison, Elbaum, Haavind, and Tinker, 2000), student engagement (Conrad and Donaldson, 2004), and authentic assessment (Palloff and Pratt, 2008). However, teaching in brick-and-mortar classrooms continues to be dominated by traditional lecture-driven modes of instruction (Cohen, Brawer, and Lombardi, 2008). Oblinger and Hawkins (2006) note that "instructors are being challenged to move beyond the notion of a course as covering content to the idea of a course as constructing a series of learning environments and activities" (p. 14). Yet instructional development training is required only for those teaching online at LMCC and for part-timers teaching online at RVCC. The assumption that full-time instructors are well versed in multiple methods of teaching is erroneous, and the decision at RVCC to require only adjunct faculty members to be trained creates a perception that adjunct faculty members who teach online are not as qualified as their full-time peers. Thus distrust exists in both institutions in regard to online education and to a greater extent at RVCC with respect to which instructors teach well in an online environment. This distrust leads to a general suspicion of the online environment in terms of teaching and learning; it has not yet been adopted as a cultural norm at either institution. It is incumbent on faculty and administrative leaders to develop trust regarding online education within their respective colleges If there is consensus that online education is good for the college and that it promotes the institutional mission and values (Hellmich, 2007).

Appropriate Use of Media

An important aspect of ethics concerns following rules and regulations. Changes in technology and types of available material cause changes in policies, guidelines, and regulations regarding how that material is used in an educational setting. That electronic materials may be used in the same ways that tangible materials have been used in physical classrooms is a false assumption (Sweeney, 2006), which bring to light ethical and legal issues as demonstrated in the following scenarios.

Scenario 3

Larry, an innovative science teacher, is developing a new online course. He attends training sessions for new online instructors and meets with an instructional technologist to plan for the course. Larry decides to incorporate PowerPoint presentations, short audio lectures, and video clips from movies with relevant themes in addition to weekly assignments and group activities. The presentations used in the online course are the same ones he uses in his face-to-face courses, which include materials gathered from various sources on the Internet. Larry also posts copies of articles that he uses in his face-to-face class that he has accumulated from various sources over the past two years. Issues of copyright and fair use were not covered during his training or in his sessions with the instructional technologist, but there is a high probability that Larry is in violation of both.

Scenario 4

Maria is contracted by her college to develop an online course that others will ultimately teach. She is given a course release and overload pay that corresponds to the credit hours for the course being developed. Rather than develop new materials, Maria chose to use presentations, practice quizzes, videos, and worksheets provided by the publisher of her textbook. Maria arranged the placement of these items in the online course and incorporated assignments and tests from her face-to-face class. Thus Maria was compensated for and provided release time to develop a course for which she did a minimum of original work.

Two related but distinct ethical issues arise from these scenarios. Both address the proper use of material in an online environment, but the first scenario concerns rules and regulations while the second concerns the type of content to be used in a course when compensation is involved. Many colleges still struggle with intellectual property and copyright issues in regard to faculty and institutional ownership, but issues of proper use may be overlooked due to the faulty assumption that the use of materials in both settings functions in the same way and is subject to the same rules.

Guidelines have long been in place for the appropriate use of copyrighted materials in the physical classroom. Fair use guidelines in the copyright law that was established in 1976 and used throughout the 1990s addressed tangible, printed material used in face-to-face classrooms (Sweeney, 2006). Updates to this law, including the Digital Millennium Copyright Act in 1998 and the Technology, Education, and Copyright Harmonization Act in 2002, were intended to clarify the use of electronic media, but they rely on a "good faith

NEW DIRECTIONS FOR COMMUNITY COLLEGES • DOI: 10.1002/cc

determination" of fair use for meeting educational objectives (Columbia University, 2008; U.S. Copyright Office, 1998). Further, guidelines for use of electronic media shared with students in an electronic environment are more restrictive than in a face-to-face situation (University of Texas, 2002). Existing guidelines have been interpreted broadly by some institutions and not at all by others, and they have been revised several times. Complicating the issue even more is the increasing use of similar technologies and media in both face-to-face and online courses. Sweeney (2006) suggests that use of media in online, hybrid, and face-to-face settings be determined on a case-by-case basis.

The implication of the scenarios, then, is that colleges must establish a norm for the use of material in electronic settings. Scenario 3 demonstrates a faculty member's earnest attempt to incorporate various media to assist student learning, but he may be in violation of copyright law. The college must determine who is responsible for ensuring proper use of electronic media, whether used online or face-to-face, and establish institutional guidelines for determination of fair use. Although faculty members may not know whether they are operating in violation of copyright law, those who are aware of the standards must do their best to stop that type of behavior for both ethical and legal reasons. Scenario 4 concerns the proper use of materials, but not from a copyright standpoint. Materials provided by textbook publishers are usually permitted for use in a physical classroom, but some publishers require students to pay a fee in order to access online material. In this situation, several factors must be considered in determining if the instructor has correctly used material for the online course. In scenario 4, the instructor is being compensated for developing a class and has chosen to use a majority of materials created by other people. Will the college knowingly pay for course materials that were created by others, or is there an expectation that faculty will be compensated for time and effort expended in creating new materials? Is it permissible to combine some original and some borrowed material, assuming that proper permissions have been obtained? Another consideration is whether the course developed is considered a "work for hire" by the college (Oblinger and Hawkins, 2006). If the course is deemed a work for hire, the college owns the copyright to the material (U.S. Copyright Office, 2004). The answers to these questions will differ by college, but clarification is needed in order for faculty members to make ethical decisions.

Discussion

Incorporating technology into education requires change. Known processes and procedures are modified, and a paradigm shift is required to accommodate new approaches to teaching and learning. The past several years have seen an increase in hybrid courses, where a significant portion of a class is taught online, and online-enhanced courses, where elements of online education such as discussion boards are incorporated into a face-to-face class.

As online education becomes more ingrained at colleges, the lines between fully online and fully face-to-face education will continue to blur. Hence it is necessary to address ethical issues in online education.

The scenarios described in this chapter illuminate the murkiness of ethical areas in online education, particularly when policies and procedures are not in place to address the issues. Of prime importance is the systemic nature of the problems. In each case, online and face-to-face education were viewed as different spheres. Certainly at some institutions, online education functions under a distance education or other extension unit that is outside of the academic realm of the college. To avoid online education's being relegated to a lower tier, trust must be established regarding the quality and importance of this type of education. A lack of trust places faculty members who teach online at a disadvantage and may also affect teaching and learning in this setting. There is a need to develop institutional awareness of laws and regulations concerning material usage in an online environment, as this affects all courses that use or store materials electronically. Institutions should also develop their own policies to guide such usage. However, creating awareness involves more than simply building a Web site or creating a policy. These guidelines must be incorporated into existing institutional practice and be openly discussed among administrators and full-time and adjunct faculty.

This chapter has touched on a small sampling of issues that have arisen with online education, but there are a host of other situations to consider. For example, course management systems allow for the collection of large amounts of data on faculty and students. How should these data be collected and used? Who should have access to them? Is it ethical to reuse material that was created by students in an online course? How can student privacy be respected while still attempting to build a community? The answers to these issues are not straightforward and may differ, depending on institutional culture and norms. Talking about these issues will ensure awareness and prompt more thinking about the ethical implications of online education.

Recommendations for Campus Leaders and Faculty Teaching

Online

- *Develop a community of trust surrounding online education.* Share information about online courses and programs with employees who do not teach online. Ensure that expectations for quality across the institution are clear.
- *Generate awareness of laws and policies that govern the usage of electronic media,* particularly when they are stored for use with a class. Ensure that existing copyright and intellectual property policies are clear and that they specifically relate to electronic materials. Gather ideas from other institutions, such as the ones listed next.

- *Have clear expectations for online faculty members.* Clarify requirements for course development, and include information about acceptable use of materials from outside sources.
- *Hold campuswide discussions about online education.* Make sure that people in all areas of the college are involved. Librarians, in particular, are key in discussions regarding information literacy. Talking about the future directions of online education may generate useful insights for future issues.

Resources

Austin Community College Copyright and Fair Use Web site: http://irt .austincc.edu/copyright

Maricopa Community College Copyright Law Tutorial: http://www.maricopa .edu/legal/ip/copyright_tutorial/copyright_tutorial.htm

Developing and Implementing Successful Intellectual Property Policies for Online Courses: http://www.mcli.dist.maricopa.edu/educause/Resources .php

Guiding Questions

1. How is online education viewed by faculty, staff, and administrators throughout your institution? Are measures in place to ensure quality of instruction for all faculty members?
2. What are your institutional policies and procedures regarding copyright and intellectual property in an online environment? Is this information readily available? How is the information shared with faculty and staff? Are new employees directed to this information, and does someone dialogue with them about this information?
3. What are the expectations for online faculty in regard to teaching? Course development? Are these expectations shared with all faculty or only those who teach online? Are expectations different for online and face-to-face instructors? Why?

References

Allen, I. E., and Seaman, J. *Staying the Course: Online Education in the United States, 2008.* Needham, Mass.: Sloan Consortium, 2008.

Barr, R. B., and Tagg, J. "A New Paradigm for Undergraduate Education." *Change,* 1995, 27(6) 13–25.

Bender, T. *Discussion-Based Online Teaching to Enhance Student Learning: Theory, Practice, and Assessment.* Sterling, Va.: Stylus, 2003.

Cohen, A. M., Brawer, F. B., and Lombardi, J. R. *The American Community College* (5th ed.). San Francisco: Jossey-Bass, 2008.

Collison, G., Elbaum, B., Haavind S., and Tinker, R. *Facilitating Online Learning: Effective Strategies for Moderators.* Madison, Wis.: Atwood, 2000.

Columbia University. "Fair Use Checklist." 2008. [http://www.copyright.columbia.edu/fair-use-checklist]. Feb. 1, 2009.

Conrad, R. M., and Donaldson, J. A. *Engaging the Online Learner: Activities and Resources for Creative Instruction.* San Francisco: Jossey-Bass, 2004.

Hellmich, D. M. "Considerations of Power, Influence, and Cultural Norms for the Ethical Community College Leader." In D. M. Hellmich (ed.), *Ethical Leadership in the Community College: Bridging Theory and Daily Practice.* Bolton, Mass.: Anker, 2007.

Meyer, K. A. "Quality in Distance Education: Focus on Online Learning." *ASHE-ERIC Higher Education Report,* 2002, 29(4).

Myskja, B. "The Categorical Imperative and the Ethics of Trust." *Ethics and Information Technology,* 2008, *10,* 213–220.

O'Banion, T. *A Learning College for the 21st Century.* Phoenix, Ariz.: American Association of Community Colleges and American Council for Education, 1997.

Oblinger, D. G., and Hawkins, B. L. "The Myth About Online Course Development: 'A Faculty Member Can Individually Develop and Deliver an Effective Online Course.'" *Educause Review,* 2006, *41*(1), 14–15.

Palloff, R. M., and Pratt, K. *Building Learning Communities in Cyberspace: Effective Strategies for the Online Classroom.* San Francisco: Jossey-Bass, 1999.

Palloff, R. M., and Pratt, K. *The Virtual Student. A Profile and Guide to Working with Online Learners.* San Francisco: Jossey-Bass, 2003.

Palloff, R. M., and Pratt, K. *Collaborating Online: Learning Together in Community.* San Francisco: Jossey-Bass, 2004.

Palloff, R. M., and Pratt, K. *Building Online Learning Communities: Effective Strategies for the Virtual Classroom* (2nd ed.). San Francisco: Jossey-Bass, 2007.

Palloff, R. M., and Pratt, K. *Assessing the Online Learner: Resources and Strategies for Faculty.* San Francisco: Jossey-Bass, 2008.

Sweeney, P. C. "Faculty, Copyright Law, and Online Course Materials." *Online Journal of Distance Learning Administration,* 2006, 9(1). [http://www.westga.edu/~distance/ojdla/spring91/sweeney91.htm]. Feb. 9, 2009.

U.S. Copyright Office. "The Digital Millennium Copyright Act of 1998: U.S. Copyright Office Summary." 1998. [http://www.copyright.gov/legislation/dmca.pdf]. Feb. 9, 2009.

U.S. Copyright Office. "Works Made for Hire Under the 1976 Copyright Act." 2004. [http://www.copyright.gov/circs/circ09.pdf]. Feb. 16, 2009.

University of Texas. "The TEACH Act Finally Becomes Law." 2002. [http://www.utsystem.edu/ogc/intellectualproperty/teachact.htm]. Feb. 9, 2009.

REGINA L. GARZA MITCHELL is assistant professor of educational leadership at Central Michigan University.

*This chapter introduces a process for inquiry that
institutions can use to dialogue about institutional
ethics. Double-loop learning involves questioning,
reflecting on, and coming to a common understanding
of institutional norms, values, policies, and ethical codes.*

7

An Inquiry Process for Individual and Institutional Ethics

Patricia L. Farrell

When Joliet College was founded in 1901, the mission of a junior or community college was simple: to offer the first two years of a four-year college curriculum to students who wanted to stay in their own communities. More than a century later, community colleges today are being challenged not only within their own walls but also by forces external to the institution. For example, in Chapter Two, Anderson, Lujan, and Hegeman note that community college personnel "are trying to balance a variety of issues, including changing student employee demographics, pedagogical and curricular shifts, advances in technology, aging physical plants, increased competition, multiple and conflicting opportunities, reliance on partnerships, mission drift, diminishing budgets, increased scrutiny and calls for accountability, and all of the other realities of today's community college world." This comprehensive list seems daunting but is easily recognized by community college practitioners.

  In this volume, my colleagues and I have set out to explore various ethical dilemmas that faculty, administrators, and staff encounter each and every day at their colleges, based on the diverse issues of the early twenty-first century. We did not attempt to address all areas or issues that might give rise to ethical dilemmas at today's community college, but we hope that the stories and vignettes presented help illuminate and explain critical ethical decisions with the goal of helping colleges explore, learn, and develop an *institutional ethical identity*, as introduced in Chapter Two.

The foundation for a successful college is framed by both institutional values exhibited in its mission, culture, structure, and organization and the way the college implements these values. Thus the college's institutional values must be real and respected. And as Schein (1996) would say, these institutional values must be some of the things that leaders embed and transmit within the culture. In their chapter, Anderson, Lujan, and Hegeman discuss the importance of clarifying the institution's mission, purpose, and values to aid in creating an institutional ethical identity. This identity is reflected in the shared beliefs, values, and assumptions and is shown "in what is done, how it is done, and who is involved in doing it" (Tierney, 1988, p. 3). Ultimately, it is reflected in the attitudes and behaviors of the personnel. The purpose of this final chapter is to outline a process explaining how college personnel can go about working collectively to learn as an organization and develop an institutional ethical identity as a whole and as subunits or departments. At the end of each chapter, we include discussion questions that college personnel can use in the process of inquiring, reflecting on, and coming together with a common understanding about ethical issues as they relate to the mission, purposes, and values of the college.

Dewey characterized traditional ethical theory as holding "the assumption of a single, fixed ideal pattern of life or a single fixed law or duty" (Garrett, 2001, p. 3). He argued instead, however, that there is a "plurality of changing, moving, individualized ends" and not a "single fixed law or duty." Therefore, college personnel need to develop "principles, criteria, [and moral] laws" for examining individual or exclusive issues (Dewey, 1982, p. 173). If we follow Dewey, it is critical for college personnel to take time to reflect deeply on the process before they act. That is, they must reflect on these changing, moving individualized ends when approaching significant issues from an institutional ethical perspective. For Dewey (1938), this is a form of inquiry, and it begins with a difficult situation, a situation that has a fundamental conflict. In this volume, we set out to focus on both individual and institutional ethics as the basis for inquiry. Inquiry combines intellectual reasoning and action, but because it is transactional, inquiry involves feelings and emotions as well. Last, following Dewey (1938), we believe that inquiry regarding institutional ethics must be continuous and open-ended.

Inquiry on Institutional Ethics

Before working as a collective to develop an institutional ethical identity, college personnel need to step back and ensure that everyone has an opportunity to understand the college's mission, purposes, and values. In this chapter, I take the next step in the process to consider how college personnel can work together to create that institutional ethical identity. I use the work of Argyris and Schön, the fathers of organizational learning, who refer to organizational learning as practice-oriented, productive, and inquiry-

NEW DIRECTIONS FOR COMMUNITY COLLEGES • DOI: 10.1002/cc

based. Their work follows in the footsteps of Dewey's writings on ethical theory and inquiry.

My starting point is Argyris and Schön's observation that individuals have "mental models or maps" operating when they encounter a situation or issue (1974). Similarly, I believe that college personnel should have analogous maps to help them plan, execute, and reflect on their actions. It is these maps that guide their actions rather than the philosophy or theory they explicitly espouse. Argyris (1980) goes on to say that few individuals are conscious of the maps they use when executing their actions. Argyris and Schön (1974) propose that there are two contrasting theories of action: theory in use and espoused theory.

Theory in use is what college personnel do; and espoused theory is the way they describe or identify their actions to others. Theory in use presides over their actual behavior and tends to be unspoken or implied (Argyris and Schön, 1974). In other words, their actions are sometimes inconsistent with their values. College personnel are often not aware of this contradiction (Gill, 2000), whereas espoused theory is expressed by the words they use to communicate their commitments or what they would like others to think they do (Argyris and Schön, 1974). Of course, in stressful times, they often revert to theory in use.

Argyris and Schön (1974) provide a model that college personnel can use to inquire and challenge individually and institutionally espoused theories and theories in use (see Figure 7.1), in their efforts toward developing an institutional ethical identity. The goal for college personnel is to lessen the gap between their theories in use and espoused theories. Therefore, for this model to be applied successfully, there needs to be a sharing of power and a process for allowing open and honest communication. The goal is to work together by maximizing the contributions of each individual. Figure 7.1 introduces the model's three variables, which will be described in detail along with recommendations for how college personnel might focus on each variable (based on Argyris and Schön, 1966).

Governing variables for action are an individual or college's values. On campus, individuals try to act within acceptable limits framed by their values. However, any action is likely to affect a number of such variables or values; therefore, any situation can trigger a trade-off among governing

Figure 7.1: Theory-in-Use Model

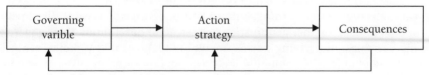

Source: Adapted from Argyris and Schön, 1974, p. 89.

variables or values. To help individuals stay within their guiding variables and make decisions, individuals need the following:

a. Sharing of valid and relevant information including feelings
b. Informed choices without coercion
c. Compelling satisfaction with and internal commitment to the decision and to the monitoring of its implementation

Action strategies are the moves and plans individuals use to keep their governing variables or values within the acceptable range. To create an ethical identity, colleges need to do the following:

a. Design situations in which individuals can be personally involved in designing and implementing sources of action
b. Agree to tasks' being jointly controlled by competent individuals
c. Ensure that self-protection is a joint enterprise and oriented toward growth

Consequences are what happen as a result of an action. The consequences can be intended or unintended. When the consequences of the action strategy are what the individual wanted, the theory in use is recognized—there is a match between intention and result. With this model in mind, and to create an ethical identity, colleges need to focus on three areas:

a. Consequences of the behavioral world
   Keeping defensiveness to a minimum
   Optimal interpersonal relations and group dynamics
   Learning-oriented norms
   Strong sense of freedom of choice, internal commitment, and risk taking
b. Consequences on learning
   Processes open to scrutiny
   Double-loop learning (to be described shortly)
   Frequent public testing of theories
c. Consequences of effectiveness
   Increased long-term effectiveness

When there is variance between the college personnel's action and the consequence, they can use either single-loop or double-loop learning (see Figure 7.2). Argyris and Schön (1966) argue that most learning happens through single-loop learning; when a consequence is in error, college personnel look at another action strategy instead of questioning their governing variables, underlying norms, mental models, values, policies, ethical codes, and objectives. Double-loop learning, however, "involves questioning the role of the framing and learning systems which underlie actual goals and strategies" (p. 22).

New Directions for Community Colleges • DOI: 10.1002/cc

Figure 7.2: Single- and Double-Loop Learning

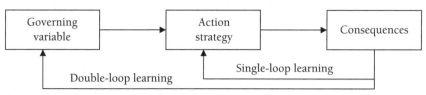

Source: Adapted from Argyris and Schön, 1974, p. 89.

In Chapter Four, Aragon and Brantmeier present an example of institutional epistemological racism along with a paradigm for analyzing racism and social dominance (Howard, 2006). Their example is of a gay faculty member presenting a new course proposal to the college's curriculum council. The faculty member proposed teaching a multicultural class on literature; however, he was told that it was too radical and that he needed to tone it down. At this institution, college people talk about diversity, but what is clear is that there is a large gap between the faculty's theories in use and their espoused theories. In this example, the council members tell the proposer of the course to come up with another action strategy, completely missing the opportunity of stepping back and scrutinizing and coming to a common understanding of what they mean by diversity. Does it mean more than racial and ethnic inclusion? How does diversity tie in to curriculum? These two questions are only examples to begin the dialogue around diversity as it relates to the college's mission, purposes, and values.

When it comes to using double-loop learning, institutional leaders need to encourage open communication while creating an environment of respect and trust where individuals can test their mental models or assumptions and beliefs (Argyris and Schön, 1996). To accomplish this, the leaders must allow ample time for the personnel involved to discuss their mental models openly, and all involved must provide valid information. In addition, all personnel need to share all the information relevant to an issue using specific examples so that other individuals can determine independently whether the information is accurate. This also means that all individuals must have an opportunity to understand the information that is being conveyed to them. Next, the personnel must allow for free and informed choice, whereby individuals make decisions on the basis of relevant and valid information and are not coerced or manipulated. Finally, leaders need to allow time for internal commitment to the choice so that individuals feel personally responsible for the decisions they make; their decisions must be compelling on their own merits rather than because individuals believe they will be rewarded or penalized for their decisions (Schwarz, 1994).

This approach helps individuals take responsibility for ensuring that decisions contributing toward an institutional ethical identity are made effectively. As a result, the participants will be more committed to the college. They will also be more receptive in the future to dialoguing and receiving information to make choices. The contributors to this volume have made it clear that college personnel need to take time and effort to use double-loop learning. Dialogue is essential because so many ethical issues are not black and white but rather fall into gray areas. Therefore, before college personnel can work together on creating an institutional ethical identity, all individuals need to work on coming together to dialogue about, agree on, and support the mission, purposes, and values of the college. An important factor in using double-loop learning is that leadership has to give up both total control of the discussion and any influence on the decisions that college personnel make in developing an institutional ethical identity.

A cautionary note is warranted, however. Leadership must be aware that in using this process for all individuals' commitment toward the college's mission and purpose, not all faculty, staff, or administrators may agree. So when a lack of agreement becomes chronic for some individuals, the question may be, "Is this person a good fit for the college?" As discussed earlier, carrying out one's espoused theories is difficult, and it takes everyone involved to ensure that the college works toward the mission and purpose of the institution.

As illustrated in each of the chapters, examining and talking about ethical issues in a community college must be ongoing because today's world is complex and ever-changing. We encourage readers to think back to the time (not that long ago) when distance education meant correspondence courses. Today, of course, the Internet and technologies associated with it such as blogs, wikis, virtual learning worlds, podcasts, and social bookmarking have transformed community colleges. These technologies have dramatically changed the ways in which community colleges deliver their programs and services and thus have introduced new ethical dilemmas for college personnel.

In conclusion, I suggest that if college leaders are serious about developing an institutional ethical identity, they should consider hiring a facilitator for the initial dialogues. A facilitator can help identify behaviors inconsistent with the ground rules or the discussion and help individuals learn effective behavior when working with groups.

Guiding Questions

1. What is your college's decision-making model? Is your college capable of using a double-loop learning model? What would the college need to change to use a double-loop learning model effectively?
2. What are your college's norms or mental models based on your mission statement?
3. What are your college's current ethical challenges? What ethical standards and boundaries are being challenged?

References

Argyris, C. *Inner contradictions of rigorous research*. New York: Academic Press, 1980.

Argyris, C., and Schön, D. A. *Organizational Learning II: Theory, Method, and Practice*. Boston: Addison-Wesley, 1996.

Argyris, C., and Schön, D. A. *Theory in Practice: Increasing Professional Effectiveness*. San Francisco: Jossey-Bass, 1974.

Dewey, J. *Logic: The Theory of Inquiry*. New York: Holt, Rinehart and Winston, 1938.

Dewey, J. "Reconstruction in Philosophy." In J. A. Boydston and R. Ross (eds.), *John Dewey and the Middle Works, 1899–1924*, Vol. 12: *Reconstruction of Philosophy and Essays, 1920*. Carbondale: Southern Illinois University Press, 1982.

Garrett, J. "John Dewey Reconstructs Ethics." 2001. [http://wku.edu/~jan.garrett/dewethic.htm]. Feb. 15, 2009.

Gill, S. J. *The Manager's Pocket Guide to Organizational Learning*. Amherst, Mass.: HRD Press, 2000.

Howard, G. *We Can't Teach What We Don't Know: White Teachers, Multiracial School* (2nd ed.). New York: Teachers College Press, 2006.

Schein, E. H. "Culture: The Missing Concept in Organizational Studies." *Administrative Science Quarterly*, 1996, *41*, 229–241.

Schwarz, R. M. *The Skilled Facilitator: Practical Wisdom for Developing Effective Groups*. San Francisco: Jossey-Bass, 1994.

Tierney, W. "Organizational Culture in Higher Education: Defining the Essentials." *Journal of Higher Education*, 1988, *59*, 1–21.

PATRICIA L. FARRELL *is the director of university outreach and policy research at the Presidents Council, State Universities of Michigan.*

INDEX

AACC. *See* American Association of Community Colleges

Access, institutional, 47–48

Acculturation mismatch, 23

ACPA. *See* American College Personnel Association (ACPA)

Akintunde, O., 42–44

Alfred, R. L., 20

Allen, I. E., 63

American Association of Community Colleges (AACC), 25, 54, 58, 59

American College Personnel Association (ACPA), 58

Anderson, S. K., 17, 19, 21, 22, 26, 56, 57, 71, 72

Aragon, A., 39, 75

Argyris, C., 72–75

Austin Community College Copyright and Fair Use Web site, 69

Baker, G. A., III, 20, 32

Baldwin, J. M., 55

Banks, J. A., 42

Banning, J. H., 19, 24

Barr, M. J., 56

Barr, R. B., 65

Bart, C. K., 24

Bastedo, M. N., 3

Bender, T., 65

Berry, J. W., 19

Biswas, R. R., 34, 35

Blackburn, S., 41

Bragg, D., 39, 48

Brantmeier, E. J., 39, 75

Brawer, F. B., 20, 27, 53, 65

Burke, J. C., 5

Callanan, P., 59

Cameron, S. C., 43

Campbell, A., 24

Carspecken, P. F., 41

Clem, B., 45

Code of ethics, developing, 25–26

Cohen, A. M., 10, 20, 27, 53, 65

Collison, G., 65

Columbia University, 66–67

"Common schools," 32

Community college institutional accountability environment: Deweyan perspective on, 5–14; nature of dilemma in, 7–9

Community College Survey, 54

Community colleges: culture, challenges, and complexities of, 19–20; ethical acculturation and culture of, 21–23; institutional decision making in, 39–49

Conrad, R. M., 65

Corey, G., 59

Corey Schneider, M., 59

Coututier, L., 5–6

David, F. R., 24

Davies, T. G., 19, 21–24, 26, 56, 57

Davis, G. W., 41

Davis, M., 25

Day, M., 5

Delpit, L., 42

Democracy, Dewey on, 10–12

Democracy in Education (Dewey), 7, 11

"Democracy's college," 9–10

Desler, M. K., 56

Developing and Implementing Successful Intellectual Property Policies for Online Courses (Web site), 69

Dewey, J., 5–14, 55, 72–73; on democracy, education, and educational aims, 10–12; implications of, for Lucero, 12–13; perspective of, on negotiating community college institutional accountability environment, 5–14

Digital Millennium Copyright Act (1998), 66

Diversity ethics, 40–41

Donaldson, J. A., 65

Double-loop learning, 74, 75

Dougherty, K. J., 6, 20, 56

Dowd, A., 9, 10, 47, 48

Durham Technical Community College, 32

Educational aims, Dewey on, 10–12

Elbaum, B., 65

Epistemology, critical: and diversity-affirming ethics, 39–49; philosophical and conceptual overview of, 41–43

Ethical acculturation, 21

79

Ethical issues: for community college student affairs professionals, 53–61; in online environment, 63–69
Ethical reasoning, developmental models for, 54–56
Ethics, diversity-affirming, 39–49; curriculum and instruction in, 44–47; and institutional access and opportunity, 47–48
Ethics Resource Center, 25
Ethos, 40
Eurocentrism, 42–44

Farrell, P. L., 71
Farris-Smith, Alice, 17, 18, 21–23, 26
Flores, R., 48
Florida, 34
Fowler, J., 55

Garrett, J., r7
Garza Mitchell, R. L., 63
Geertz, C., 19
Gill, S. J., 73, r7
Gilligan, C., 55
Gollattsheck, J. F., 20
Gottlieb, M. C., 19, 21–23
Grant, C. A., 40
Grubb, W. N., 2
Guglielmino, L., 20
Gumport, P. J., 33

Haavind, S., 65
Habermas, J., 55
Hagan, B., 48
Handelsman, M. M., 19, 21–23
Harbour, C. P., 5, 6, 10, 19, 21–23, 26, 39, 48, 56, 57
Harding, S., 19
Hawkins, B. L., 65, 67
Hegeman, D. L., 17, 19, 24, 71, 72
Helfgot, S. R., 53–54
Hellmich, D. M., 53, 63–65
Herring, D., 33, 36
Hickman, L. A., 10
Hines, C. T., 34
Hong, E., 6
Hornak, A. M., 53
Howard, G., 41, 42, 46, 75

Ingram, W. G., 31
Institutional ethical identity, 72; and acculturation mismatch, 23; and clarifying institution's mission, purpose, and values, 24–25; creating opportunities for, 23–26; and culture, challenges, and complexities of community college, 19–20; and developing code of ethics, 25–26; and ethical acculturation, 21–23; importance of professional and, 17–27
Institutional ethics, community college: and diversity-affirming ethics and critical epistemology, 39–49; and ethical dimensions of open-door admissions policy, 31–37; and importance of professional and institutional ethical identity, 17–27; inquiry process for individual and, 71–76; and negotiating institutional accountability environment, 5–14; in online environment, 63–69; and student affairs professionals, 53–61

Jaquette, O., 5, 10, 48
Johnston, J. S., 10
Joliet College, 71
Junior colleges, 32

Kegan, R., 55
Kelly, J. B., 35
Kidder, R., 31, 36
King, P. M., 55
Kitchener, K. S., 55
Knapp, S., 19, 21–23
Kohlberg, L., 55
Komives, S. R., 56

Ladson-Billings, G., 42
Land-grant colleges, 32
Lazerson, M., 12
Locke, M. G., 20
Lombardi, J. R., 20, 53
Lucero, L., 7–10; Deweyan implications for, 12–13
Lujan, L., 17, 71, 72

Maricopa Community College Copyright Law Tutorial, 69
Martin, J., 20
Martin, Q. S., 35
Maslow, A., 55
Massachusetts, 33
Mead, G. H., 55
Media, appropriate use of, 66–67
Medsker, L., 32
Meritocracy, 42

Meyer, K. A., 65
Mission, institutional, 24–25
Modern Language Association, Committee on Community Colleges, 44
Moral reasoning, developmental models for, 54–56
Morrissey, S. E., 31
Mountain and Plains Community College (MPCC), 7–9, 12, 13; Humanities and Learning Community (HLC) program, 7, 9, 13; real estate licensure (REL) program, 7
MPCC. *See* Mountain and Plains Community College (MPCC)
Myskja, B., 64

NASPA. *See* National Association of Student Personnel Administrators (NASPA)
National Association of Student Personnel Administrators (NASPA), 58
"New Guidance on the Admission of Undocumented Individuals" (Sullivan), 34
New Mexico, 34
New York, 33
Newman, F., 5–6
Noddings, N., 55
North Carolina, 33–36; General Statutes, 34
North Carolina Community College System (NCCCS), 33–36
North Carolina State Board of Community Colleges, 35
North Suburban Community College (NSCC), 17, 18, 26
NSCC. *See* North Suburban Community College (NSCC)

O'Banion, T., 65
Oblinger, D. G., 65, 67
Online education: and appropriate use of media, 66–67; ethics in, 63–69; issues of trust in, 64–65; recommendations for campus leaders and faculty teaching concerning, 68–69; resources for ethics in, 69
Open-door admissions policy, ethical dimensions of, 31–37
Opportunity, institutional, 47–48

Palloff, R. M., 65
Pappas, G. F., 10, 11

Pendergraph, J., 35
Perry, W. G., 54–55
Piaget, J., 55
"Positive freedom," 11
Pratt, K., 65
Purpose, institutional, 24–25

Rawls, J., 49
Recommended Code of Ethics for Chief Executive Officers of Community Colleges (American Association of Community Colleges), 25
Rhoads, R. A., 48
Roueche, J. E., 32
Ryan, A., 11

Sam, D. L., 19
Schein, E. H., 19, 20, 72
Scheurich, J., 43, 46
Schön, D. A., 72–75
Schwarz, R. M., 75
Scurry, J., 5–6
Seaman, J., 63
Shapiro, J. P., 55–58
Shugart, S. C., 32
Single-loop learning, 74, 75
Sleeter, C. E., 40
Spring, J., 46
Standards of Professional Practice (NASPA), 58
Stanfield, J. H., 43
Starratt, R. J., 54
Stefkovich, J. A., 55–58
Student affairs professionals: and community college students, 53–54; and developmental models for ethical and moral reasoning, 54–56; and ethical decision making, 59–60; ethical issues for, 53–61; ethical responsibilities for, 56–57; practitioner scenarios for, 57; profession of, 56; and professional codes and standards, 57–59
Sullivan, D., 34
Suppiger, J. E., 20
Sweeney, P. C., 66, 67

Tagg, J., 65
Tate, W. F., IV, 42
Technology, Education, and Copyright Harmonization Act (2002), 66
Texas, 33, 34
Theory-in-use model, 73–74
Tierney, W., 72
Tinker, R., 65

Truman Commission Report, 47–48
Trust, issues of, 64–65

United States Department of Homeland
    Security, 35
University of Chicago, College of Education, 10
University of Texas, 67
U.S. Copyright Office, 66–67
U.S President's Commission on Higher
    Education, 47–48

Valadez, J. R., 48
Values, institutional, 24–25

Vaughan, G. B., 6, 19, 20, 31
Virginia, 34

Wallin, D., 41
Wattenbarger, J. L., 20
Westbrook, R. B., 10, 11
Wiggs, J. L., 34
Wildes, K. W., 18, 19
Witt, A. A., 20
Woodard, D. B., Jr., 56
Woody, W. D., 19, 20
Wycoff, S. M., 43

Young, M., 43, 46